IT ALL ADDS UP

Math Skill-Building Activities for Grades

by Denise Bieniek, M.S.
Illustrated by Dan Regan

Troll
CREATIVE
TEACHER
IDEAS

Troll Creative Teacher Ideas was designed to help today's dedicated, time-pressured teacher. Created by teachers for teachers, this innovative series provides a wealth of classroom ideas to help reinforce important concepts and stimulate your students' creative thinking skills.

Each book in the series focuses on a different curriculum theme to give you the flexibility to teach any given skill at any time of the year. The wide range of ideas and activities included in each book are certain to help you create an atmosphere where students are continually eager to learn new concepts and develop important skills.

We hope this comprehensive series will provide you with everything you need to foster a fun and challenging learning environment for your students. **Troll Creative Teacher Ideas** is a resource you'll turn to again and again!

Titles in this series:

Classroom Decor:
Decorate Your Classroom from Bulletin Boards to Time Lines

Creative Projects: Quick and Easy Art Projects

Earth Alert: Environmental Studies for Grades 4-6

Explore the World: Social Studies Projects and Activities

Healthy Bodies, Healthy Minds

Holidays Around the World: Multicultural Projects and Activities

It All Adds Up: Math Skill-Building Activities for Grades 4-6

Learning Through Literature:
Projects and Activities for Linking Literature and Writing

Story Writing: Creative Writing Projects and Activities

Think About It: Skill-Building Puzzles Across the Curriculum

The World Around Us: Geography Projects and Activities

World Explorers: Discover the Past

Metric Conversion Chart

1 inch = 2.54 cm	1 foot = .305 m	1 yard = .914 m
1 mile = 1.61 km	1 fluid ounce = 29.573 ml	1 cup = .24 l
1 pint = .473 l	1 teaspoon = 4.93 ml	1 tablespoon = 14.78 ml

Contents

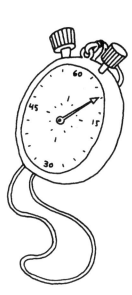

Fairy Tale Survey

JACK AND THE BEANSTALK | **SNOW WHITE** | **HANSE** | **THREE BEARS**

Brainstorm with the class about fairy tales. Encourage the students to name as many different stories as they can remember. When everyone is done, ask each student to name his or her favorite fairy tale.

Show the class's favorites in graph form. Write the names of the favorites across the bottom of a large sheet of butcher paper or oaktag. Attach the sheet to a bulletin board.

Give each student a 2" x 4" piece of construction paper. Ask students to fold the paper in half to resemble small books and then write their names on the fronts.

Read the name of the first fairy tale title aloud. Ask students who have named that fairy tale as their favorite to come to the board and glue their "books" on the graph above the title. Make sure the students line the books up one above the other with as little space between the books as possible. Then move on to the other titles listed on the graph.

Compare and contrast the number of books in each column. Which title received the most votes? Which title received the fewest? Which titles have half the number of votes as others? Are any fairy tales better liked by boys than girls, or vice versa?

If desired, take the survey idea to the rest of the school. Ask the teacher of each class to spare five minutes while a member of your class polls their students to find out their favorite fairy tales and records how many boys and girls voted for each one.

When all the votes are in, complete a graph for each grade level. Color in the graphs instead of making construction paper books. Are there different favorites in each grade, or do the same titles appear again and again? Do the boys or girls in each grade seem to like one particular tale? Overall, which fairy tale got the most votes? Publish or post the results for the school.

Rumpelstiltskin Riddles

Name _____

Find the answers to these measurement questions. For each problem, draw a diagram illustrating the relevant information.

1. The miller's daughter was led into a dingy rectangular room. One side was 3' across and covered with slimy moss. Another side was 14' across and had names of past prisoners scratched into the stone. What is the perimeter of this room?

_____

2. The miller's daughter cried and cried until a funny little man appeared. He offered to spin the straw into gold for her. When the king saw all the gold, he put the miller's daughter into a larger room, filled with even more straw. If the room measures 20' long, 13' wide, and 8' high, how much straw, in cubic feet, can fit in the room?

_____

3. In the third room were baskets lined up on every wall from floor to ceiling, just brimming with straw. The miller's daughter thought there had to be at least 100 pounds of straw in each basket. If the total weight of the baskets is 6,045 pounds, and there are 139 baskets, how much does each basket weigh? Round your answer to the nearest ones place. Then convert your answer to kilograms. (Hint: A kilogram weighs 2.2 pounds.)

_____

4. The king decided to marry the miller's daughter after she had spun the last of the straw into gold. He lavished on her gifts of jewels, dresses, and entertainment. Her castle bedroom measured 40' long and 30' wide. The dressing room measured 20' long and 16' wide. The sitting room measured 50' long and 45' wide. Her bath measured 10' long and 10' wide. What is the area, in square feet, of each room?

_____

5. A daughter was born to the queen and king. Soon thereafter, Rumpelstiltskin came to collect his fee for having spun the straw into gold. The queen begged for three chances to guess his name, and the little man agreed. The queen sent out her best messengers to find out the name of every person in the kingdom. Together, they rode 67 miles that day. The next day, the messengers rode 80 miles. The third day, the messengers rode 95 miles. If there were 5 messengers each day, each riding the same number of miles, how many miles did each messenger ride the first, second, and third days? How many miles total did each messenger ride?

_____

Shoemaker's Size Chart

sk students to call out their shoe sizes. Have two students record the information on a chalkboard.

Ask everyone to write the sizes down on a piece of paper in order from smallest to largest. When sizes are duplicated, tell students to include each entry in the ordering.

Ask volunteers to explain how to find the average of a group of numbers. Remind the class that an average is the sum of two or more quantities divided by that number of quantities. To find the average shoe size of the class, they must add all the sizes up and divide by the number of sizes they added. Ask students if they feel the average is an accurate description of their shoe sizes.

Next, have the class figure out the median shoe size of the class. Ask if anyone knows how to find the median. To find the median, students must find the size having the same number of sizes larger than it as smaller than it. If there is an even number of sizes, students should find the size that is between the two middle sizes. How close is this shoe size to the average shoe size? Do students think this is a more accurate method for finding the size that most of the class wears?

Find the mode of the shoe sizes. Ask if anyone can explain how to do this. Inform the class that to find the mode, they must identify the size most often given. How does mode compare with the other two methods? Which of the three methods do students think is best for finding the shoe size most students wore? What would happen if one fifth-grade class was composed of large children and another was filled with smaller children? Would using the mode to find the most common shoe size for that grade be a fair method? Which of the three would be the best method?

Have students predict the answer to this question: Is there a relationship between height and shoe size? Call out the shoe sizes in order, from smallest to largest, and have students call out their height when their shoe size is called. Students can write the heights next to the shoe sizes on their original lists. Ask them to compare and contrast height and shoe size and check their predictions.

Testing Averages

Help!

Name _____

Help this teacher figure out the averages for each student in the class. Write the answers on the lines provided at the bottom of the cards.

Alex
Math	86
Spelling	94
Science	98
History	91
Writing	89
	___

Sam
Math	
Spelling	
Science	78
History	100
Writing	82
	90
	94
	___

Jessica
Math	92
Spelling	84
Science	88
History	96
Writing	90
	___

Ray
Math	
Spelling	100
Science	72
History	92
Writing	90
	84
	___

Kate
Math	100
Spelling	100
Science	98
History	96
Writing	97
	___

Denise
Math	
Spelling	87
Science	99
History	90
Writing	82
	93
	___

Chris
Math	
Spelling	
Science	75
History	86
Writing	88
	82
	87
	___

Jamie
Math	99
Spelling	87
Science	96
History	94
Writing	92
	___

What is the average for the entire class? _____

Beanstalk Measurements

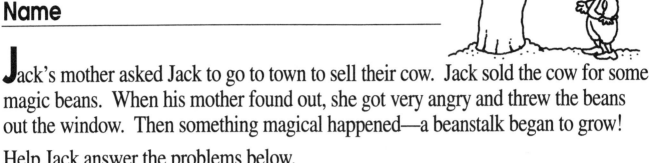

Name _____

Jack's mother asked Jack to go to town to sell their cow. Jack sold the cow for some magic beans. When his mother found out, she got very angry and threw the beans out the window. Then something magical happened—a beanstalk began to grow! Help Jack answer the problems below.

1. The morning after Jack's mother threw the beans out the window, a beanstalk was 3" high. How many feet high is the stalk? _____

2. Later that same day, Jack noticed the stalk was even taller. In five hours, the stalk had grown 9" more. How many inches is the stalk? _____ How many yards is the stalk? _____

3. During the night, the stalk grew 5 feet higher. Convert the 5 feet to inches and then to centimeters.
_____

4. What is the total height of the stalk so far in inches, feet, and yards? _____
_____

5. By the end of the second day, the stalk had reached 6,000 feet. How many yards is that?
_____

6. On the fourth night, the stalk had reached 3 1/2 miles in height. Jack decided to climb it the next morning. By dawn, the stalk had grown another mile. Jack figured he could climb at least half the stalk. How many meters will Jack be climbing?
_____

7. By the time Jack reached the end of the stalk, he had climbed some 9,240 yards. How many miles had Jack climbed? _____

8. When Jack reached the top, he read a sign that said, "Giant's Castle—62 kilometers ahead." The next sign read, "Beware—You are 17 kilometers from the Giant's Castle." The last sign read, "Go Back While You Still Can!—Only 2 more kilometers to the Giant's Castle." How many meters distance was there between the first and second signs? _____
Between the second and third signs? _____

Energy Costs

Name _____

Use the chart to figure out how much Rosa's family must pay to run their new air conditioner.

| Room Air conditioner 8,000 BTU/hr | | | A-a-a-h So Cool! Model #51068 | |

ENERGY RATING
10.0
This Model
How much to run per year?

Cost per kilowatt hour:	Yearly hours of use:			
	250	750	1,000	2,000
2¢	$3	$9	$12	$24
4¢	$6	$18	$24	$48
6¢	$9	$27	$36	$72
8¢	$12	$36	$48	$96
10¢	$15	$45	$60	$120

1. If Rosa's family uses their air conditioner for 750 hours a year and their electric company charges 4 cents per kilowatt hour, how much will their bill be? _____

2. How much will it cost to use the air conditioner for 500 hours at 6 cents per kilowatt hour? _____

3. If they use their air conditioner for 3,000 hours per year at a cost of 12 cents per kilowatt hour, how much will they be billed? _____

4. If there was a column for 500 hours of yearly use, what would the costs be for 2 cents, 4 cents, 6 cents, 8 cents, and 10 cents per kilowatt hour? _____

_____

5. Figure out what it would cost Rosa's family to operate their air conditioner for 500, 1,250, 1,500, and 1,750 yearly hours of use at 8 cents per kilowatt hour. What pattern do you see as you scan across the 8-cent-per-kilowatt-hour row? _____

6. What pattern do you see down the 250-yearly-hours-of-use column? _____

Patterns in Nature

Name _____

Find the patterns in the nature problems below.

1. You are experimenting with growth serums on Venus's-flytraps in your greenhouse. The following data has been collected on growth for the past two weeks:

2 cm	4 cm	16 cm	256 cm	65,536 cm

What pattern can you see in the numbers listed on the data sheet? _____

2. Charlie is building a robot that can move forward when an electrical impulse is generated. The first day's work yields a forward movement of 2". The next day, the robot moves 7". The following week's data looks like this:

22"	67"	202"	607"	1,822"

What pattern do you see in the robot's movement? _____

3. The following numbers were printed out when a pattern formula was typed into the computer. The numbers generated were these:

$$1, 3, 9, 27, \ldots 6,561.$$

What are the numbers missing from this pattern? _____

4. After a forest fire, seedlings were planted to help reforest the area. After the first year, the trees were 3' high. After the second year, the trees were 4' high. After the third, fourth, and fifth years, the trees were 6', 9', and 13' high. How tall will the trees be after the tenth year?

_____

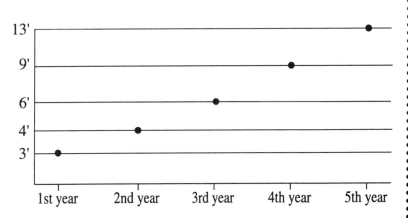

5. You have been watching a herd of sea lions for a few years now. When the observations began, there were 66 sea lions. They doubled in population each year for 6 years. How many sea lions are there by the end of 6 years?

_____

Calorie Counting

65 calories!

Name _____

Answer the following questions about calories.

1. You have heard the saying, "An apple a day keeps the doctor away." What if you ate one apple, at 65 calories each, every day for a year? How many calories would you consume? _____

2. An average-sized woman should consume 1,200 calories a day. If an average-sized woman has the following foods for breakfast, what percentage of calories is left for the rest of her meals? _____

    plain tea—0 calories
    rye toast with butter—123 calories
    scrambled egg—79 calories
    grapefruit—44 calories

3. The calories in a piece of green pepper (4 calories) are what fraction of the calories in 2/3 cup of raspberries (64 calories)? _____

4. Which salad contains fewer calories? _____

Vegetable Salad	Fruit Salad
lettuce—18 calories	apple—65 calories
mushrooms—15 calories	blueberries—68 calories
onion—21 calories	grapes—74 calories
cucumber—7 calories	strawberries—41 calories
tomatoes—23 calories	honeydew melon—48 calories
radishes—7 calories	

5. What is the difference in calories between the two salads? _____

6. Two men who are friends consume different amounts of calories each day. Ted eats approximately 2,035 calories a day. Ned consumes approximately 2,100 calories a day. Ted weighs 185 pounds, and Ned weighs 175 pounds. What is the ratio of calories to weight for each man?

_____

7. If 3/4 cup blackberries has 57 calories, how much would 1/2 cup have? _____

1/4 cup? _____ A whole cup? _____

Math Combinations

Name _____

Work out the answers to the problems below. Show your work on a separate sheet of paper. Use the back of this sheet if you need extra space.

1. Six people are at a party. If each person shakes everyone else's hand, how many handshakes will there be?

_____

2. Tamika has four shirts, five pairs of pants, and three different pairs of shoes in her closet. How many combinations of outfits can she make with them? _____

3. Ricky has five different-colored toy cars in his toy box. How many different four-color combinations of cars does Ricky have?

_____

4. Mom is serving rice, chicken, and two types of beans for dinner. How many different dinner combinations can be made using at least two of these foods? _____

5. There are 43 animals registered in the pet show. Some are four-legged, some are two-legged, and some have no legs. There are three times as many two-legged animals as four-legged animals. If there are a total of 100 legs, how many animals have four legs? _____

How many have two legs? _____

How many have no legs? _____

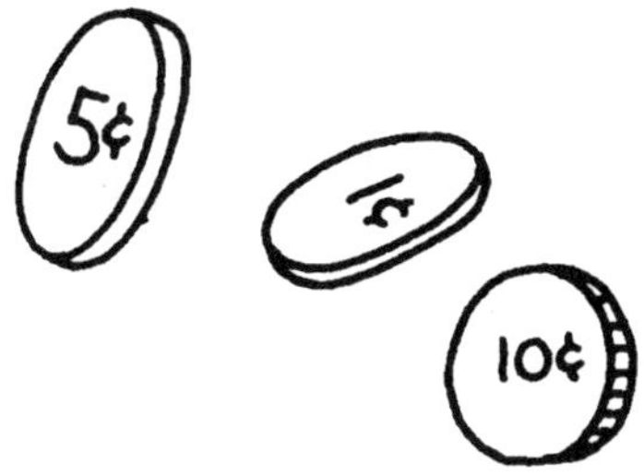

6. How many combinations of pennies, nickels, and dimes would give you 21 cents? _____

Questions and Answers

Name _____

Write a question for each set of facts given. Make sure the problems make sense. Then exchange your questions with a classmate and try to answer his or her questions while he or she tries to answer yours.

1. Trudy makes $3.75 an hour at the Burger Barn, and Jill makes $3.60 an hour at the Potato Ranch. They both work 15 hours a week. _____

_____

2. Samuel runs 3 miles a day. Each mile takes him 5 minutes to run. His sister Beth can run 4 1/2 minute miles. _____

_____

3. Angie swims 1 hour every day. Her friend Tom swims 2 hours once a week. The number of laps they swim each session is the same. _____

_____

4. Apples are selling for $2.45 a pound in the city and $1.50 a pound in the countryside.

_____

5. The most expensive sneakers in the store have just gone on sale. Fifteen people are waiting outside the doors the morning of the sale. There are twelve pairs of sneakers left at the sale price.

_____

6. Chrissie is 49 years old, Max is 27 years old, Patrice is 14 years old, and Tillie is 7 years old.

_____

7. A seed is planted at the beginning of summer. Two months later, the plant is 12" tall.

_____

8. For the barbecue, Sal bought a watermelon at $3.59, a package of hot dogs at $4.24, hot-dog buns for $.99, chips at $.89, and a bottle of juice for $2.78. _____

_____

Group Word Problems

Divide the class into groups of three. Instruct the groups that they will need a piece of paper and a pen for this activity. The student in each group who is the youngest will be the recorder; the student who is the oldest will be the reader; and the middle student in each group will be the checker (who will make sure everyone in the group agrees on various points and everyone stays on task).

Write a set of facts about any topic on the chalkboard and ask the readers to read the facts to their groups. For example, "It takes an average fifth-grade class of 28 students five minutes to walk from their room to the gym. It takes a kindergarten class of 18 students ten minutes to walk from their class (next to the fifth-grader's class) to the gym."

When the checker has made sure everyone in his or her group knows the facts, ask the groups to create as many questions as they can based on those facts. The recorder will write down all the group's questions on the sheet of paper.

When ten minutes are up, ask the reader in each group to read one question from his or her group's list. Tell the readers that you are looking for a different question from each group. See how many rounds you can do before the questions begin to sound alike. For homework, ask students to answer the questions they wrote. Allow time for them to copy the questions into their notebooks.

The next day, have students break up into their groups again and compare their answers. If there are disagreements, encourage students to explain their processes and answers. When a group agrees on all their answers, ask the recorder to write out one copy of their questions and answers to hand in for checking.

Students may also wish to make a book with the questions they created. Each question may be written on a large index card, with the answer written on the back. All the cards may then be stapled together along the left side or along the top to make a book. Place the book in the math center for use during free time. The index cards may also be stored in a file box instead of in book form.

Home Cooking Conversions

Name _____

Use measuring cups, spoons, and containers to experiment with water. Then fill in the chart below. Answer the questions based on information in the chart.

_____ teaspoons	=	1 tablespoon
_____ teaspoons	=	4 tablespoons
_____ tablespoons	=	1/4 cup
_____ cups	=	1 pint
_____ pints	=	1 quart
_____ quarts	=	1 gallon
_____ cups	=	1 gallon
_____ ounces liquid	=	1 cup

1. How many cups equal one quart? _____

2. How many tablespoons equal 1/2 cup? _____
   3/4 cup? _____ 1 whole cup? _____

3. How many cups equal 12 ounces of water? _____

4. How many cups equal 10 pints? _____

5. How many ounces of water are in 1 gallon? _____

6. How many teaspoons equal 1 cup? _____

Homemade Fudge Brownies

MATERIALS:

1/2 cup butter or margarine at room temperature
1 cup sugar
1 teaspoon vanilla
2 eggs
2 one-ounce squares of unsweetened chocolate, melted
1/2 cup sifted flour
extra butter
mixing bowl
wooden spoon
8" x 8" cake pan

DIRECTIONS:

1. Place 1/2 cup of butter, 1 cup of sugar, and 1 teaspoon of vanilla in a mixing bowl. Beat them until well blended.
2. Beat in 2 eggs.
3. Blend in two melted 1-ounce squares of unsweetened chocolate.
4. Stir in 1/2 cup of flour. Do not overstir; the batter should be slightly lumpy.
5. Grease an 8" x 8" cake pan with butter. Spoon the batter into the pan and smooth it until level.
6. Bake at 325°F for about 30 minutes.
7. When the brownies have cooled, cut them into squares. Enjoy!
Yield: approximately 16 squares

Doughnut Rounds

MATERIALS:

2 eggs
1/4 cup sugar
1 teaspoon salt
2 tablespoons melted shortening
1/3 cup milk
1 1/2 cups flour
4 teaspoons baking powder
bottle of vegetable oil
lunch bags
1 cup confectioner's sugar

DIRECTIONS:

1. Beat 2 eggs in a mixing bowl until well blended.
2. Add 1/4 cup of sugar, 1 teaspoon of salt, 2 tablespoons of melted shortening, and 1/3 cup of milk to the eggs. Beat well.
3. Mix 1 1/2 cups of flour and 4 teaspoons of baking powder in a separate bowl. Combine the two mixtures.
4. Fill a deep, heavy pot halfway with vegetable oil. Heat the oil to approximately 375°F. Gently place three or four doughnut rounds, 1 tablespoon each, into the hot oil and fry for about 3 minutes, or until golden brown.
5. Place the rounds on a paper bag to drain and drop the next batch of doughnut rounds into the oil. Fill a paper lunch bag with 1 cup of confectioner's sugar and place the first rounds inside. Close the top and shake gently.
6. Place sugared doughnut rounds onto a plate. Continue frying and coating with sugar until all the dough is finished. Enjoy!
Yield: approximately 30 doughnut rounds

Sewing Skills

So, sew!

Name _____

Answer the questions based on the information given in the chart.

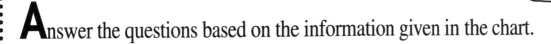

	Sizes—Fabric Needed (in yards)								
	1	**2**	**3**	**4**	**5**	**6**	**7**	**8**	**9**
VIEW A	1 1/2	1 1/2	2	2 1/2	3	3 1/8	3 7/8	4	4 1/4
VIEW B	2	2	2 1/2	3	3 1/4	3 7/8	4	4 1/2	5
VIEW C	1	1	1 1/2	1 3/4	2	2 1/4	2 3/4	3	3 1/4

NOTIONS: VIEW A—1/2 yd elastic, 1 yd ribbon; VIEW B—5 buttons; VIEW C—2 buttons
SUGGESTED FABRICS: cotton, damask, chambray, poplin, corduroy

1. How much fabric would you need if you were sewing View B for a size 8 person?

_____

2. To sew two View A shirts, one for a size 2 and one for a size 6, how much fabric would you need?

_____

3. What type of notions do you need to complete View C? _____

4. If there were only 2 yards of fabric left on the bolt, and you were making View C, size 4, would there be enough fabric? _____

5. If you used a whole yard of ribbon for a View A, size 6 shirt, how much would you need for a View A, size 3 shirt? _____ A size 12? _____

6. How many View C shirts could you make with 5 1/2 yards of fabric? Identify one combination of sizes. _____

7. If you were making a View B shirt for each of your 24 cousins, how many buttons would you need? _____

8. How much fabric would you use if you were making a View A shirt and needed a size between sizes 8 and 9? _____

Name _____

You have just moved to a new home, and your parents have told you that you may decorate your room any way you like. Answer the following questions about measurement.

1. You need fabric to make a pillowcase for a 16" x 20" pillow. You must leave 1/2" extra all around on the front and the back in order to have room for sewing the seams of the case. How much fabric will you need to buy for your pillowcase?

_____

2. The next project you want to do is to build shelves for your room. You want shelves 6' long and 12" deep. When you go to the lumber store, you find they sell boards of the following dimensions: 3' long x 4" deep, 3' long x 8" deep, 3' long x 12" deep; 4' long x 4" deep, 4' long x 8" deep, 4' long x 12" deep; 5' long x 4" deep, 5' long x 8" deep, 5' long x 12" deep. What would be the easiest combination of boards with which to build your shelves?

_____

3. Now you must figure out how to lay tile in the bathroom. If the room is 8' long and 6' wide, and the tiles you want are 1 square foot, how many tiles will you need to cover the floor? If there are 12 tiles in each box, how many boxes will you need to buy?

_____

4. You are going to make curtains for your windows. One window is 45" wide and 71" tall. The other window is 33" wide and 71" tall. The directions on the pattern package tell you that the width of the fabric you will need must be triple the width of the window. Your fabric is 54" wide. If you want to cover both windows whole, and remembering that you'll need the extra 1/2" seam allowance on all sides, how many yards of fabric should you buy?

_____

5. Staining a desk for your room is next. The desk will need about 1 quart of stain for a first coat and the same for a second coat. The containers of stain are sold in gallon sizes. After the two applications, how much stain will you have left over?

_____

6. You want your lamp to be in a particular corner of the room, but the outlet is in the opposite corner. You will need to buy an extension cord. The hardware store sells them in 6', 8', 10', 15', 18', and 20' lengths. If your room dimensions are 10' x 8 1/2', and the cord will run along the base of the walls, how long a cord should you buy?

_____

Buying Lumber

Name _____

$\mathbf{A}$nswer the questions based on information given in the chart below.

WOOD PRICE CHART				
Depth		**Width**	**Length**	**Price**
2"	x	4"	6'	$2.00
			9'	$2.30
			12'	$2.60
1"	x	3"	6'	$1.40
			8'	$1.60
			10'	$1.80
1"	x	6"	6'	$2.00
			10'	$2.50
			12'	$3.00
1"	x	12"	6'	$3.75
			10'	$4.50
			12'	$5.25
Wallboard				
1"	x	4'	6'	$10.00

1. You are building a deck that measures 24' wide and 15' deep. Your plan is to buy 2" boards that are 6' and 9' in length to cover the 15' depth. How many boards of each size will you need to buy to cover the 24' width? _____

2. You want to build a bookcase 3' high, 3' wide, and 6" deep, having an open front and back and one shelf in the middle. How many boards and what size will you need to buy? What will it cost you?

_____

3. You must complete one wall in a play house. It will require some wallboard. The wall is 6' high and 10' wide. How many pieces of wallboard will you need to cover the wall? _____
Will there be any left over? _____ How much? _____

4. How much would it cost if you bought the following items: two 10', 1" x 3" boards; three 12', 1" x 12" boards; three wall boards? _____ Round your answer up to the next dollar. Now add 5% sales tax. What would be your new total? _____

5. Could you buy a piece of lumber at the store that is 1" deep, 3" wide, and 9' long? How much would you have to saw off the next sized board to get this size? _____

Does It Fit?

Name _____

Copy the apartment and its dimensions, given below, onto graph paper, using a scale of 1' equals 1 box. Use a second piece of graph paper to cut out furniture for the apartment, using the same scale as the house. Then answer the questions based on the information given.

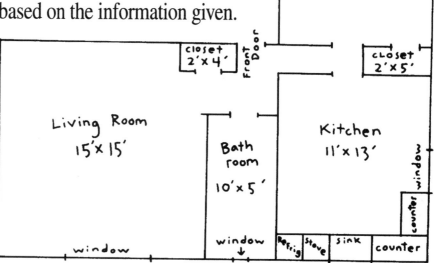

1. How could you arrange the living room with the following furniture:

6' x 3' couch	4' x 3' loveseat
2' x 3' coffee table	1' x 2' television stand
5' x 2' piano	1 1/2' x 1 1/2' coat rack

2. Would your 7' x 7' king-sized bed fit in the bedroom? _____ Could you also fit a 3' x 2' dresser, a 4' x 2' desk, a 1' x 2' night table, and a 2' x 2' chair in the bedroom? _____

3. If the tub in the bathroom is 5' x 3', the toilet takes up 2' x 2', and the sink takes up 2' x 1 1/2', how big a rug could you buy for the bathroom floor? _____

4. How might you arrange a 4' x 3' table, four 1 1/2' x 1' chairs, and a 2 1/2' x 1 1/2' microwave cart?

   _____

5. If you were going to buy wall-to-wall carpeting for the living room, bedroom, and hallways, how many total square feet would you need to buy? _____

6. On a separate piece of graph paper, draw three connecting rooms in your home to scale. Share the drawing with the class.

Supermarket Sales

Name _____

Answer the shopping questions below. Show your work.

1. The 40-ounce box of your favorite laundry detergent is on sale for $4.99. The same detergent is available for $9.99 in a 100-ounce bulk size. Which size box costs less per ounce?

_____

2. The dishwashing detergent in the 22-ounce bottle will wash 46 sinkfuls of dishes. How much would the 96-ounce bottle wash?

_____

3. The 22-ounce bottle of dishwashing detergent costs $2.88, and the 96-ounce bottle costs $7.50. How much per sinkful does it cost to use each of these products? Round off your answers.

_____

_____

4. How many ounces of detergent are used per sinkful of dishes? Round off your answer.

_____

_____

5. You have arrived at your vacation spot for one week of fun and relaxation. There is a kitchen available, so you decide to cook your own meals. When you go to the supermarket, your favorite cereal is being sold in a 10-ounce box for $3.68. The same cereal is also sold in a 20-ounce box at a 30% discount. If the sticker on the shelf under the 20-ounce box reads 39 cents per ounce, what is the normal cost of the product? What will your total be with the discount?

_____

_____

6. In aisle 4, ice cream is on sale. If you buy more than two containers, you will receive 25% off the purchase price. Normally, the ice cream sells for $2.66 a container. If your purchase comes to $9.97, how many containers of ice cream did you buy? Round your figures to the nearest hundredths as you work.

_____

Automobile Shopping

Name _____

You have finally saved enough money to buy yourself a car. Answer the car-shopping questions below. Show your work.

1. You're trying to decide between two cars, one costing $3,000 and one costing $3,400. The first car gets 12 miles to the gallon; the second car gets 20 miles to the gallon. You drive approximately 9,000 miles a year, and gas is averaging $1.19 a gallon. How much would it cost to run each car for one year? Which car would be the least expensive at the end of one year, including the purchase price?

_____

2. Would your answer be the same after two years? How much would each car cost at the end of two years?

_____

3. A new car with standard features, such as an air bag, a radio, automatic transmission, and manual windows, will cost $14,800. To get extras, such as a compact disc player, air-conditioning, a passenger-side air bag, and antilock brakes, will cost more. Each feature adds 5% of the list price to the total price of the car. How much would the car cost with just one extra feature? With all four?

_____

4. How many features would have to be added for the total cost of the car to come to $20,720?

_____

5. You are offered a car loan for $12,000 at 7% interest for three years. You will be responsible for sending a monthly payment to the bank. How much will the total cost of the loan be, including interest? How much will your monthly payments be? Round your figures to the nearest dollar.

_____

6. The warranty on the car you want to buy covers it for just one year. However, you can purchase the extra-protection plan for $480 a year for a minimum of four years, which would be figured into your costs when you bought the car. If you buy the plan, how much will it cost?

_____

You're Invited!

Name _____

Help the staff at Perfect Party Planners figure out the problems below. Answer the questions on the lines provided, and show your work on another piece of paper.

1. There will be 8 people at a party, all bringing gifts for each other. How many gifts will be brought to the party? _____

2. There will be 14 people at a party, and you need to figure out how much soda to buy. You figure each person will have 16 ounces to drink. Soda bottles come in a 1-liter size. How many liters of soda will you need? How many bottles will you need to buy? (Hint: 1 liter equals 33.8 ounces.) _____

3. You have been asked to provide cups for another party. The host has bought 96 ounces of juice and asked you to get 3-ounce cups. How many 3-ounce cups of juice will be available at the party? If everyone can have two cups, how many people are at the party? _____

4. The first party of the season had 35 guests. The second party had 12 guests, and the third had 28 guests. What was the average number of guests at the three parties? If the fourth party had triple the average number, how many guests were there? _____

5. At a party to start off the school year, there were 258 students and 6 chaperons. What was the ratio of students to chaperons at the party?

_____

6. The biggest party of the year had so many guests that there was only about 4 square feet of space for three people. If the room measured 148 square feet, how many people were there? _____

Vacation Time

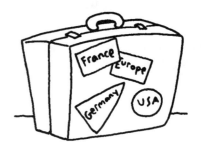

Name _____

It's vacation time! Figure out the answer to each of the travel problems below. Remember to show your work on a separate piece of paper.

1. You get plane tickets two months in advance for $299. One month later, you see the same tickets offered by another airline for less than what you paid. The penalty for canceling tickets is $35. Would it be worth canceling if the other airline's tickets cost 2/3 what the first airline's cost? What would be the total cost of the second set?

_____

2. Filling up your car at a gas station, you read a sign telling you that credit card payment will cost an additional 3 cents per gallon. Having only a credit card, you fill the tank anyway. If you receive 16 gallons of gas, and the total cost comes to $20, how much was the price per gallon? How much would the total have been if you had paid in cash?

_____

3. Create a circle graph showing the following information about a 20-day trip: 3 days at the beach, 5 days sightseeing, 1 day sick, 1 day on a farm, 1 day of travel, and 9 days visiting relatives and friends.

_____

4. When traveling in Europe, you notice the metric system is used. One kilometer is equal to approximately 5/8 of a mile. If you traveled 3 kilometers on the first day, 16 on the second, and 8 on the third day, approximately how far in miles would you have gone?

_____

5. You have brought the family car with you for your stay in Germany. The car gets 18 miles to the gallon. If the car has 1 gallon of gas left in the tank, and you are 17 kilometers from Berlin, can you make it to Berlin without buying gas?

_____

6. You have decided to rent bicycles when you reach the country. At the rental shop, you find 1/4 of them are red, 1/5 are green, 1/10 are blue, 3/10 are orange, and 3/20 are yellow. Convert the fractions into percentages. Which color is the most popular?

_____

Balancing the Books

Name _____

Read the bank book entries below. Compare the entries with the bank statement on the next page. Draw up a new bank book page showing the corrections needed.

Check #	Date	Transaction	Debit	Credit	Balance
					1,000.00
	5/1/94	Withdrawal ATM	20.00		20.00
					1,980.00
120	5/10/94	to Dr. Bean	60.00		60.00
					2,040.00
	5/16/94	Deposit		200.00	200.00
					2,240.00
121	5/24/94	to Electric Company	21.45		21.45
					2,218.55
122	5/25/94	to Telephone Company	63.95		63.95
					2,154.60
	6/1/94	Withdrawal ATM	60.00		60.00
					2,094.60
123	6/10	to Mary Lane	45.23		45.23
					2,049.37
	6/16/94	Deposit		92.37	92.37
					2,141.74
	6/20/94	Withdrawal	100.00		100.00
					2,041.74
125	6/29/94	to Electric Company	23.72		23.72
					2, 018.02
126	6/30/94	to Telephone Company	54.63		54.63
					1,963.39
	7/2/94	Deposit		80.00	80.00
					2,043.39
	7/6/94	Withdrawal	60.00		60.00
					1,983.39

Balancing the Books

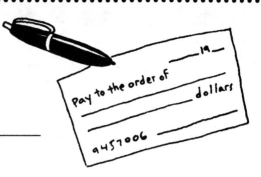

Name _____

BANK STATEMENT			
Beginning May 1, 1994 and Ending July 7, 1994			
			1,000.00
5/1/94	**Withdrawal**	20.00	20.00
5/10/94	**Check # 120**	60.00	60.00
5/16/94	**Deposit**	200.00	200.00
5/20/94	**Withdrawal**	20.00	20.00
5/24/94	**Check # 121**	21.45	21.45
5/25/94	**Check # 122**	63.95	63.95
6/1/94	**Check # 123**	650.00	650.00
6/1/94	**Withdrawal**	60.00	60.00
6/10/94	**Check # 124**	45.23	45.23
6/16/94	**Deposit**	92.37	92.37
6/20/94	**Withdrawal**	100.00	100.00
6/29/94	**Check # 125**	23.72	23.72
6/30/94	**Check # 126**	54.63	54.63
7/1/94	**Withdrawal**	20.00	20.00
7/2/94	**Deposit**	80.00	80.00
7/6/94	**Withdrawal**	60.00	60.00
			End Balance $173.39

Top Ten Hits

Name _____

Answer the questions about the top singles based on the information in the chart. Remember to show your work on a separate piece of paper.

NUMBER THIS WEEK	NUMBER LAST WEEK	TITLE	ARTIST
1	3	Put Your Hand in Mine	Terry Shane (Jazz)
2	1	Oh, Baby!	Conan (Pop)
3	5	Love Is Grand	Bobby Silver, Jr. (Blues)
4	2	Shades	Tia Perez (Pop)
5	6	Time to Cry	Boyd Lane (Rap)
6	4	Heartbreak	Jack and the Rabbits (Blues)
7	7	Ray of Sunshine	The Blobs (Jazz)
8	10	Hairy Days and Nights	Bob E. Pin (Rap)
9	8	Time Outdoors	Patty O'Furniture (Pop)
10	9	Riding in My Car	The Racers (Rock)

1. What percentage of last week's top five artists stayed in the top five? _____

2. Which type of music consistently moved down on the charts? _____

3. Create a Venn diagram of the titles that moved up, moved down, and stayed the same. Mark one circle "Up," one circle "Down," and the overlapping area "Stayed the Same."

4. The path of the new number-one single was as follows: When it hit the charts, it came in twenty-eighth, moved to 25 the following week, 18 the next week, 15 the next week, 10 the next week, 6 the next week, 3 last week, and number 1 this week. Create a line graph showing the progress of "Put Your Hand in Mine."

5. What is the average number of points "Put Your Hand in Mine" moved up the charts each week? Round off the answer to the nearest whole number. _____

6. What percentage of the singles stayed the same from last week to this week? _____
What percentage moved up? _____ What percentage moved down? _____

Musical Arrangements

Name _____

Answer the questions to the musical problems below. Remember to show your work on a separate piece of paper.

1. You are going on a trip and want to take some cassettes along. Your cassette case is 4 1/2" wide and 20" long. Your cassettes are 1" wide and 4" long. How many cassettes can you pack in the case?

_____

2. You have just bought a new stereo system. The dimensions of the boxes are:

     Box 1—18" long, 18" wide, and 7" high
     Box 2—18" long, 18" wide, and 12" high
     Box 3—18" long, 18" wide, and 20" high

If the trunk of your car measures 6 1/2 cubic feet, will the boxes fit? (Hint: 1 cubic foot = 1,728 cubic inches.) _____

3. Your album shelf measures 1 yard wide and 1 1/2 feet high. If albums measure 12" in width and height and are 1/2" thick, how many albums can you fit in one row on the shelf? _____

4. You want to tape a compact disc (CD) onto a cassette. The tracks on the CD last an average of 3 minutes and 30 seconds. Cassettes come in 45-, 60-, 90-, and 100-minute lengths. If there are 13 tracks on the CD, which size cassette should you use? _____

5. Ten songs on your new CD are less than 4 minutes long; four songs are over 5 minutes; three songs are less than 3 minutes long; three songs are exactly 4 1/2 minutes long. What percent of the CD is less than 4 minutes long? _____ Over 5 minutes? _____ Less than 3 minutes? _____ Exactly 4 1/2 minutes long? _____

6. Sam has double the number of cassettes Bill has. Bill's number of cassettes is a prime number. Kathy's cassettes are equal in number to 1/8 of Hal's collection. Hal has one less cassette than Bill, and the number of Hal's cassettes equals the square of 4. How many cassettes does everyone have?

_____

Hundreds Chart Configurations

whoooo can do these?

Name _____

Look at the box configurations below. Each problem is a group of boxes taken from a hundred square. Write the numbers in the blank squares that surround each filled-in square of a hundred square.

1.

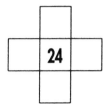

24

2.

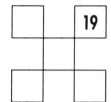

19

3.

88

4.

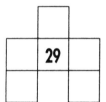

29

5.

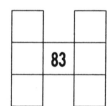

83

6.

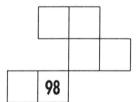

98

7.

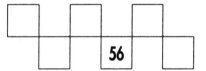

56

8.

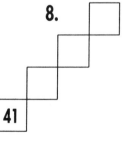

41

9.

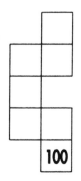

100

10.

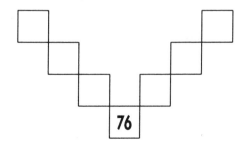

76

Hundreds Chart Configurations

Name _____

Reproduce and distribute the hundred square to each student to check their answers for the puzzles given on page 31.

1	2	3	4	5	6	7	8	9	10
11	12	13	14	15	16	17	18	19	20
21	22	23	24	25	26	27	28	29	30
31	32	33	34	35	36	37	38	39	40
41	42	43	44	45	46	47	48	49	50
51	52	53	54	55	56	57	58	59	60
61	62	63	64	65	66	67	68	69	70
71	72	73	74	75	76	77	78	79	80
81	82	83	84	85	86	87	88	89	90
91	92	93	94	95	96	97	98	99	100

Probability Activities

Heads/Heads	Tails/Tails	Heads/Tails	Tails/Heads

To begin to understand probability, students will need to practice collecting data, taking samples, organizing data, analyzing it, and making inferences from it. To gather information, both facts and opinions, students can brainstorm on strategies. Surveys, questionnaires, casual questioning, census research, and other ideas should be discussed.

Collecting data that involve opinions needs a more involved strategy. The people students poll must be unbiased, or the results of their collection will not be random. Students can learn through their polling that a sample of a population can represent the whole population if the polling is done randomly. They will also learn that some samples will need to be done nonrandomly. For example, if they wish to know how much time fathers and sons spend together each week, they would not need to poll mothers and daughters.

To organize and analyze data, students will need to make graphs, condense information, and make comparisons. When they have done the above tasks, they can begin to decide the probability of a situation. Probability helps in making predictions about whether an uncertain situation is possible or not. Explain to students that they can predict probability more accurately when they have obtained information about a subject, organized it, and analyzed it.

Ask students what the probability of rolling a three on a die would be. Explain that there are six sides on a die and the number 3 appears once, so the probability of rolling a 3 is 1/6, or 1 out of 6 chances. Ask students what the probability of rolling a 2 would be (also 1/6).

Perform the following activity with the class to help students understand probability better. Show the class a coin. Ask them how many outcomes are possible when the coin is tossed (2). Ask them how many there will be if two coins are tossed (4). Choose a student to write down the four outcomes on the chalkboard, leaving a space next to each one. Have the class predict the probability of tossing heads–heads, tails–tails, heads–tails, and tails–heads (1/4). Ask four students to toss the coins once, one after each other. The recorder should make a mark next to the outcome after each toss. If the students predicted each outcome would come up once in four tosses, were they right? What would happen if they repeated the experiment 20 more times?

Place ten large beans in a paper lunch bag. Without the students seeing, use nail polish or a small sticker to mark half of the beans so they appear different from the others. Present the bag to the students and tell them how many beans are in the bag and that there are two types of bean. Ask a student to write *Bean 1* and *Bean 2* on the chalkboard, one label under the other. Ask another student to take one bean from the bag and tell the class what it looks like, then put it back in the bag. The recorder will then make a check next to *Bean 1*. Go around the room, repeating the procedure ten more times and marking the results next to the labels on the chalkboard. Ask students to predict how many beans in the bag are plain and how many are marked, based on the data on the chalkboard. Repeat the experiment ten more times, and ask students to check their predictions. Then open the bag and see how many predicted correctly.

Estimation Activities

Hmmm...

Name _____

Estimate the following quantities. On the lines provided, explain how you came to your conclusion. Then figure the actual measurements and calculations to see how close your estimates were.

1. How tall is the person sitting next to you? _____
_____

2. What is the perimeter of your desk (table)? _____
_____

3. How many marbles could fit into one of the containers in the room? _____
_____

4. How many hands wide is the classroom? _____
_____

5. How much would eight cans of juice cost if one can costs $1.79? _____
_____

6. How many students are in your school? _____
_____

7. How many kernels of unpopped popcorn could fit in an 8-ounce cup? _____
_____

8. How many bites does it take to eat an apple? _____
_____

9. What is the circumference of your friend's head? _____
_____

10. How much does your book bag weigh? _____
_____

11. 395 + 402 + 438 = _____
_____

12. How many words are on this page (numbers don't count)? _____
_____

Tangram Puzzles

MATERIALS:

    crayons or markers
    glue
    oaktag
    scissors

DIRECTIONS:

1. Reproduce the tangram on page 36 once for each student. Have each child color each piece of the tangram any color he or she wishes.

2. Ask each student to mount his or her tangram on oaktag, cut it out, and then cut apart the individual tangram pieces.

3. Explain to the class that a tangram is an ancient Chinese puzzle. It consists of a square divided into five triangles, a square, and a rhomboid. Tangrams may be assembled to make many new figures.

4. Reproduce the tangram puzzles on pages 37–38 once for each student. See if students can use their tangrams to fill in the puzzles.

5. Ask students to come up with their own tangram puzzle designs, using their tangram pieces on light-colored paper. Have them trace around the outside edges of their tangram puzzles onto their papers. When the tangram pieces have been removed from the paper, they may use a marker to darken the outline. Bind all the designs into a book and leave it in the math center for students to use during free time.

35

Tangram Puzzles

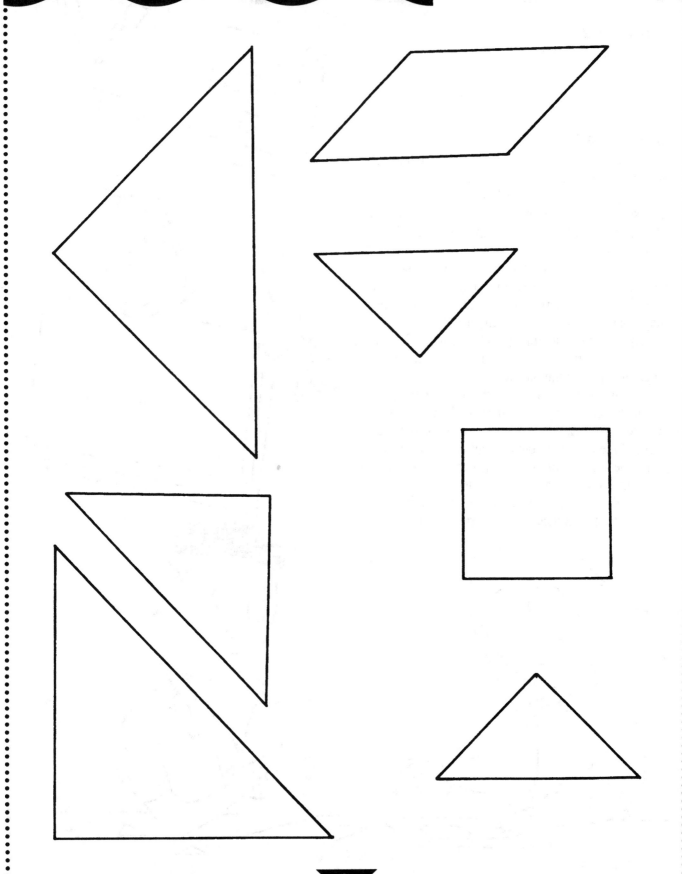

Tangram Puzzles

Name _____

Try to cover the dalmatian below using all seven tangram pieces.

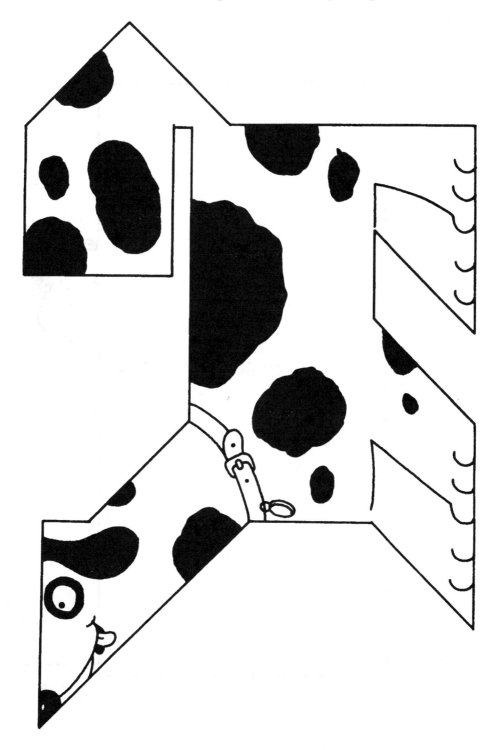

Tangram Puzzles

Name _____

Try to cover Mike's door using all seven tangram pieces.

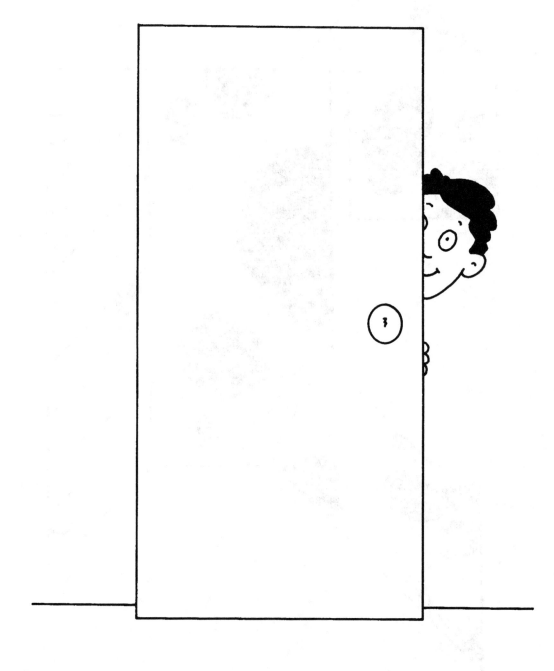

Supermarket File-Folder Game

MATERIALS:

crayons or markers
scissors
letter-sized file folder
glue
oaktag
clear contact paper
die
envelope

DIRECTIONS:

1. Reproduce the game board on pages 40–41 once. Reproduce the money, store items, and playing pieces on pages 42–43 six times. Color all the components.
2. Cut out the game board and glue it to the inside of a letter-sized file folder. Then glue an envelope to the back of the file folder to use as a storage place for the money, playing cards, and playing pieces.
3. Reproduce the "How to Play" instructions on this page. Cut them out and glue them to the front of the file folder.
4. To make the money, store items, and shopping cart playing pieces, mount them on oaktag, laminate them, and cut them out.

HOW TO PLAY:

(for two to six players)
1. The player who rolls the highest number goes first. Play continues clockwise. Place the store items along the game board shelves according to category. Each player receives two $10 bills and three $5 bills. Place the remaining money to the side.
2. Have each student roll the die six times and use the following information to make up his or her shopping list. Students should write down the type of product and the price.

> 1 = dairy product
> 2 = meat
> 3 = bread
> 4 = vegetable or fruit
> 5 = baking supply
> 6 = canned good

> dairy product costs $2.00
> meat costs $4.00
> bread costs $1.00
> vegetable or fruit costs $3.00
> baking supply costs $2.00
> canned good costs $3.00

3. When all the shopping lists are completed, play begins. The first player rolls the die and moves his or her shopping cart forward the number shown.
4. If a player lands on a spot in front of a shelf holding an item on his or her shopping list (even an Accident spot), that player may take the item from the shelf and place it in front of him or her. A player may take only one item each turn. If a player lands on an Accident spot, he or she must pay the amount shown to the store manager.
5. When a player gets all the items listed on his or her shopping list, he or she may move toward the Cashier. When a player lands on the Cashier spot, he or she must pay the total cost on the items and tell how much change should be given. (It is not necessary to land on the Cashier spot on an exact roll.) The first player who checks out correctly wins.

Supermarket File-Folder Game

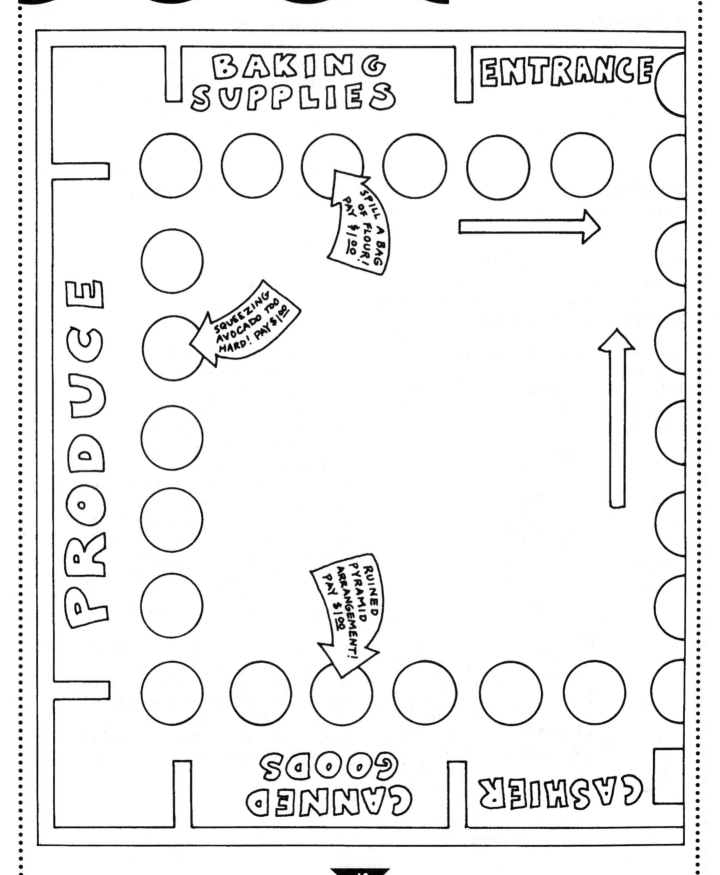

Supermarket File-Folder Game

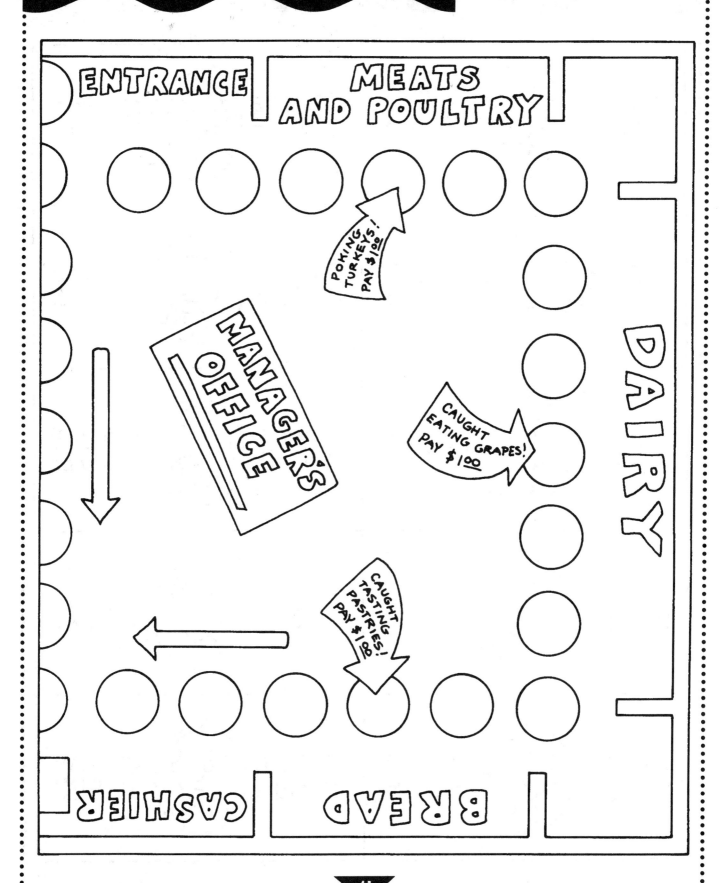

ENTRANCE

MEATS AND POULTRY

DAIRY

MANAGER'S OFFICE

POKING TURKEYS! PAY $1.00

CAUGHT EATING GRAPES! PAY $1.00

CAUGHT TASTING PASTRIES! PAY $1.00

BREAD

CASHIER

Supermarket File-Folder Game

Supermarket File-Folder Game

Coordinate Dot-to-Dot

Name _____

Plot the x and y coordinates in the box below on the graph. Connect the points in the order in which you plotted them.

1. 1,4
2. 3,6
3. 2,8
4. 5,7
5. 7,9
6. 7,6
7. 9,4
8. 6,4
9. 5,2
10. 4,4

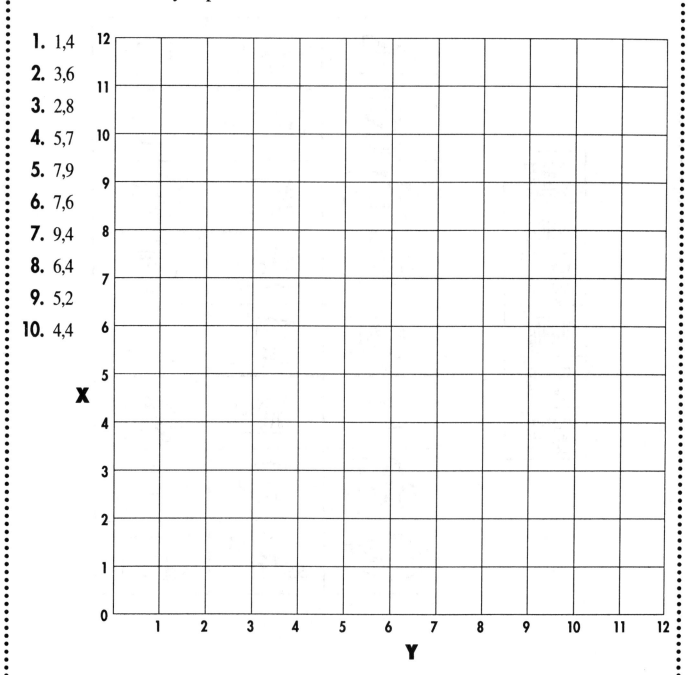

What have you drawn? _____

Place Value

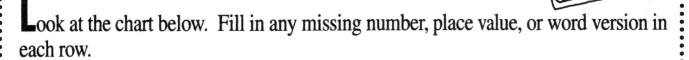

Name _____

Look at the chart below. Fill in any missing number, place value, or word version in each row.

Number	Place Value					Word Version
	Ten thousands	Thousands	Hundreds	Tens	Ones	
1. 4,809						
2.						four hundred three
3. 34,965						
4.	3	5	8	0	6	
5.		3	0	0	1	
6. 7,906						
7.						six thousand twenty-two
8. 63,840						
9.			2	9	8	
10.						fifty-nine

Mathematical Puzzle

Name _____

Solve the equations and write the answers in the boxes to complete the crossword puzzle.

Across
3. 99 x 33
5. 30,297 + 7,341
6. 89 x 245
8. 36,134 divided by 58
11. 555 squared
12. 3 to the third power
15. the hundredth number in the pattern 3, 6, 9, 12 . . .
16. 290,662 - _____ = 225,226
18. 747 1/2 + 649 1/2

Down
1. 34,098 - 27,896
2. 14,603 - 12,836
4. 87,098 + 56,003
7. 1,234 x 1,234
9. 11 x 9,876
10. the square root of 100
13. 2 to the fourth power
14. 951 squared
17. the hundredth number in the pattern 5, 10, 15, 20 . . .

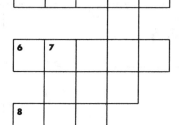
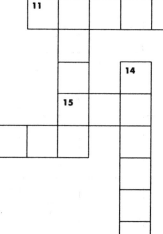
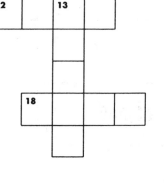

Mathematical Word Search

Name _____

Find the mathematical words hidden in the puzzle below and circle them. The words may be written forward, backward, up, down, and diagonally.

```
S T U V M A N A B S G C U S T R A T I O N M S E
U D E N T S M A T Y H N F A M P E R C E S T N R
D S U C A B A O B M D Z I R C H E R A N S T E I
E C S K U B U F A M I R N T P E R I R M E T E N
M A R G A I D C N E A N E Y R R L E S C U S U T
I U O P N K S G I T G O S V L O T T M A C M N E
M V T N E C R E P R R I B D C T S Y A R B E T G
A I C S I O N O N Y A T K V A A T V S E Y R S E
L O A B A C U M C A P C O P N L U O R S E T T R
N R F C E N T E R L I A O C T U A S F A C A A A
S E I R O E H T A P D R M I R C B A B Y M E T T
J T C E N T S R T D I F E O T L R T I I O B I O
E E T O G E T Y I O V N I R C A M I T A F S S S
T M M O C H Y T G N I T N U O C R S O W R T T T
V I A B L R I W R C S E F U N D E C I M A L I H
D R A O B O E G A P I Y A R D S S N S C C A C E
S E R A N I N K P R O B A B I L I T Y I T T S N
B P D Y B E I E H D N O I T C A R T B U S I S E
T G E O P L A N E S T A N G R U P S B R A K C S
```

abacus	diagram	geoboard	probability	addition
division	geometry	sorting	calculator	estimate
graph	statistics	decimal	Eratosthenes	integer
subtraction	fraction	ratio	patterns	symmetry
counting	percent	perimeter	theories	Cuisenaire rods
factors	numbers			

Find the 30s

Name _____

Be the first to find the row in which all the answers are between 30 and 39.

$1748 \div 46$	$\dfrac{560}{18}$	$14 \times 2 \times 1$	9×5	$\begin{array}{r} 17 \\ \times\ 3 \\ \hline \end{array}$	$89 \div 3$
$\dfrac{6}{8} = \underline{\quad}\%$	$6 \times 2 \times 3 \times 1$	$7 + 33$	$53 - 27$	$79 - 22 - 30$	$22\overline{)578}$
$698 \div 33$	$80 \div 2 \div 3$	$6\frac{1}{2} \times 4\frac{3}{4}$	4×8	$\frac{1}{3} = \underline{\quad}\%$	$7 + 33$
$69 \div 3$	$32 - 2 \times 1$	$90 - 44$	$192 \div 6$	30×0	$2 \times 4 \times 3$
$49 - 3 \times 3$	$\sqrt{841}$	$14 + 15$	$63 - 36$	$3687 - 3652$	2^3
$6\overline{)72}$	14×5	$\begin{array}{r} 36 \\ +\ 4\frac{1}{2} \\ \hline \end{array}$	7^2	3^2	$\sqrt{1089}$

Favorite Foods Survey

Divide the class into groups of five. Ask the groups to discuss favorite foods. When the students have all settled on their favorites, ask a student from each group to be a recorder and write down each member's favorite. Ask another member of each group to share their information with the class.

Inform the class that they will be making circle graphs to organize the data they have collected. Ask a third member of each group to be the graph maker. A fourth member should be picked to ensure that each member of his or her group understands the process and stays on task. The fifth member may encourage other members to join in the graph making. Remind students that they all must agree on how to make the graph and what it should look like.

Explain to the groups that they will need to show the data from each of the other groups as well as their own. They must first decide on food-group names so that each favorite food will fit in a category on the graph. Some suggestions for food-group name labels: Protein, Fats, Junk Food, Breads and Carbohydrates, Dairy, and Fruits and Vegetables. Encourage students to create food-group categories on their own.

When the groups have their categories, they must decide how many foods should be placed in each one. Then they can decide how much of a "slice" to assign each category, based on that category's percentage of the total number of foods represented in the graph. Encourage the groups to draw their slices as accurately as possible. For example, if 50% of the group like junk food best and 30% like breads, the bread slice should be smaller than the junk-food slice.

When the groups have finished, ask the recorder to hold up the graph while the reader shares his or her group's work with the class. Allow time for questions and comments after each group has shared. Display the graphs on a classroom wall or a bulletin board along with health-ful-eating tips and nutrition guidelines.

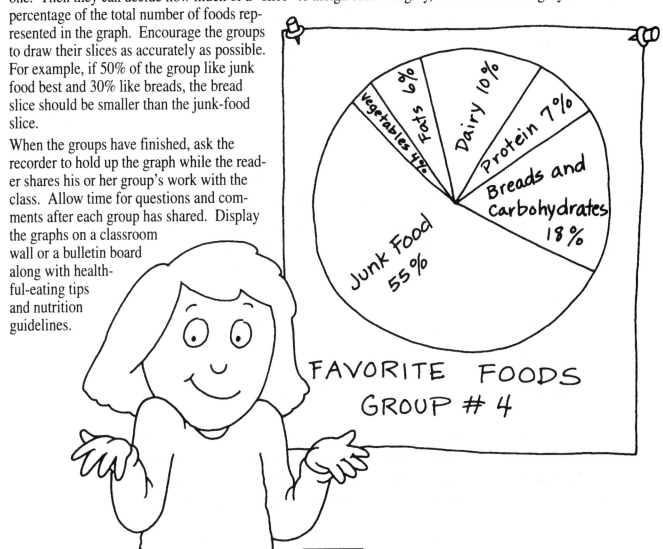

FAVORITE FOODS GROUP # 4

Time Travel

Name _____

Solve these problems about time. Remember to show your work on a separate piece of paper.

1. To travel to the local library from your home takes 30 minutes. To travel from school to your home takes 15 minutes. If you walked from school to home and then to the library, what percentage of an hour would you spend traveling?

_____

2. It takes you 50 minutes to walk the hiking trail the first week, 47 minutes the second week, 40 minutes the third week, and 30 minutes the fourth week. What is your average hiking time for the four weeks?

_____

3. You fall asleep in the year 1996 and wake up a decade later. What year is it when you wake up? How many hours have gone by?

_____

4. You have traveled to a planet known to very few people. When you arrive, you are 11 years old. As each Earth year passes, your body ages faster than it would on Earth. After the first year, you have the body of a 12-year-old. After the second year, you have the body of a 14-year-old. After the third year passes, you have the body of a 17-year-old. At the end of the fourth year, your body has aged to 21 Earth years old.

How can you express this pattern of aging? _____

How old will you be after ten years on the planet? _____

5. Your family decides to take a car trip. Along the way, the car falls into a time crater. By the time you make it back, your watch says January 30, 2103. You left on March 24, 1999. How much time has passed?

_____

6. Traveling to your cousin's place on Planet Z, you find that Planet Z's time is different from Earth's. For every Earth hour, 80 minutes pass on Planet Z. What is the ratio between the passing of time on Planet Z and the passing of time on Earth?

_____

Symmetry in Architecture

Name _____

Symmetry is an equal arrangement of parts on both sides of a dividing line. Circle the homes below that have symmetry. Then draw a line showing each home's line of symmetry.

Small-Town Ratios

Name _____

Figure out the correct ratio in each problem. Reduce the ratio to its lowest terms.

1. In Centreville High School, there are 460 students. One-fourth are taking Japanese, two-fourths are taking Russian, and the other fourth chose not to take a language. What is the ratio of students taking Russian to the number of students in the school? _____

2. In the big football games of the season, the junior varsity team scored 39 points against their opponents, and the varsity team scored 78 points. What is the ratio of junior points to varsity points?

_____

3. If the opponents' total points for both games was 120, what was the ratio of total points scored by the home teams to total points scored by the opponents? _____

4. For the ninth-grade field trip, 98 ninth-graders brought in their permission slips. There are a total of 164 ninth-graders in the school. What is the ratio of ninth-graders attending the trip to those not attending the trip? _____

5. Millie is having a big sale over at the hardware store. She has marked the finishing nails down from 38 cents a pound to 35 cents a pound, and the 2" screws from 45 cents a pound to 40 cents a pound. What is the ratio between the markdown of nails and the markdown of screws?

_____

6. In an opinion poll, 60% of the townspeople rated the new movie below a 5 on a scale of 1 (very bad) to 10 (excellent), while 30% rated the new movie above a 5. But 10% did not see the movie. What is the ratio of people who liked the movie to people who did not like it? _____

Timed Tests

Name _____

See how many of the 100 math problems below you can complete in three minutes. Ready, set, multiply!

1. 2 x 3 =	**26.** 4 x 4 =	**51.** 9 x 3 =	**76.** 12 x 0 =
2. 6 x 6 =	**27.** 11 x 6 =	**52.** 11 x 12 =	**77.** 8 x 1 =
3. 4 x 8 =	**28.** 5 x 7 =	**53.** 12 x 3 =	**78.** 3 x 11 =
4. 9 x 1 =	**29.** 1 x 2 =	**54.** 3 x 7 =	**79.** 6 x 3 =
5. 1 x 0 =	**30.** 3 x 4 =	**55.** 7 x 10 =	**80.** 9 x 10 =
6. 5 x 9 =	**31.** 7 x 11 =	**56.** 5 x 0 =	**81.** 12 x 12 =
7. 7 x 7 =	**32.** 10 x 5 =	**57.** 4 x 12 =	**82.** 8 x 5 =
8. 12 x 1 =	**33.** 8 x 7 =	**58.** 11 x 9 =	**83.** 2 x 4 =
9. 10 x 10 =	**34.** 12 x 10 =	**59.** 9 x 7 =	**84.** 5 x 8 =
10. 4 x 6 =	**35.** 9 x 9 =	**60.** 5 x 12 =	**85.** 9 x 12 =
11. 3 x 9 =	**36.** 3 x 0 =	**61.** 7 x 0 =	**86.** 7 x 6 =
12. 6 x 7 =	**37.** 6 x 9 =	**62.** 11 x 8 =	**87.** 11 x 7 =
13. 9 x 5 =	**38.** 8 x 6 =	**63.** 2 x 6 =	**88.** 8 x 2 =
14. 1 x 11 =	**39.** 11 x 4 =	**64.** 4 x 10 =	**89.** 4 x 1 =
15. 7 x 3 =	**40.** 6 x 2 =	**65.** 10 x 8 =	**90.** 2 x 10 =
16. 6 x 12 =	**41.** 1 x 7 =	**66.** 3 x 8 =	**91.** 6 x 11 =
17. 8 x 9 =	**42.** 8 x 12 =	**67.** 7 x 9 =	**92.** 3 x 3 =
18. 11 x 2 =	**43.** 10 x 11 =	**68.** 10 x 7 =	**93.** 7 x 8 =
19. 5 x 4 =	**44.** 5 x 6 =	**69.** 12 x 5 =	**94.** 10 x 4 =
20. 9 x 11 =	**45.** 2 x 7 =	**70.** 9 x 2 =	**95.** 4 x 7 =
21. 8 x 3 =	**46.** 7 x 4 =	**71.** 12 x 9 =	**96.** 1 x 10 =
22. 12 x 7 =	**47.** 10 x 3 =	**72.** 8 x 11 =	**97.** 7 x 2 =
23. 1 x 8 =	**48.** 1 x 5 =	**73.** 3 x 5 =	**98.** 11 x 10 =
24. 2 x 9 =	**49.** 6 x 4 =	**74.** 2 x 12 =	**99.** 12 x 4 =
25. 10 x 0 =	**50.** 5 x 11 =	**75.** 5 x 2 =	**100.** 4 x 9 =

Math Class Chart

DIRECTIONS:

1. Give the timed math test on page 53 each morning. Have students exchange papers and grade each other's work.

2. Make a large oaktag chart with each student's name in a column down the left side of the chart. Write column headings from left to right with numbers from 1 to 20.

3. Record the score each student receives each day on the chart. Emphasize to the class that what matters is not what score each child starts with, but rather the rate at which each student improves. Go over the scores with the class and name a student or students "Most Improved" for the day.

4. If desired, create a new set of more challenging problems for students to do after they have received scores of 100 on the timed test on page 53.

Multiplication Bulletin Board

DIRECTIONS:

1. Choose one of the pairs of patterns on pages 56–59 (football helmet and football, or rocket and shooting star) to use for a multiplication facts bulletin board. Reproduce the selected patterns 12 times each for the multiplication facts, then as many times as necessary to make a border for the designated area of the bulletin board.

2. Color the patterns and cut them out. Make a border for the bulletin board, as shown.

3. Write out a set of multiplication facts (for example, 4 x 0 = 0, 4 x 1 = 4, 4 x 2 = 8) on strips of paper. Place the strips vertically on the bulletin board, as shown. Write the answer for each fact on a football or a star, depending on the theme chosen.

4. When the class has learned the entire set of multiplication facts, put a new set on the board. Continue until the students have memorized all sets of multiplication facts from 1 through 12.

55

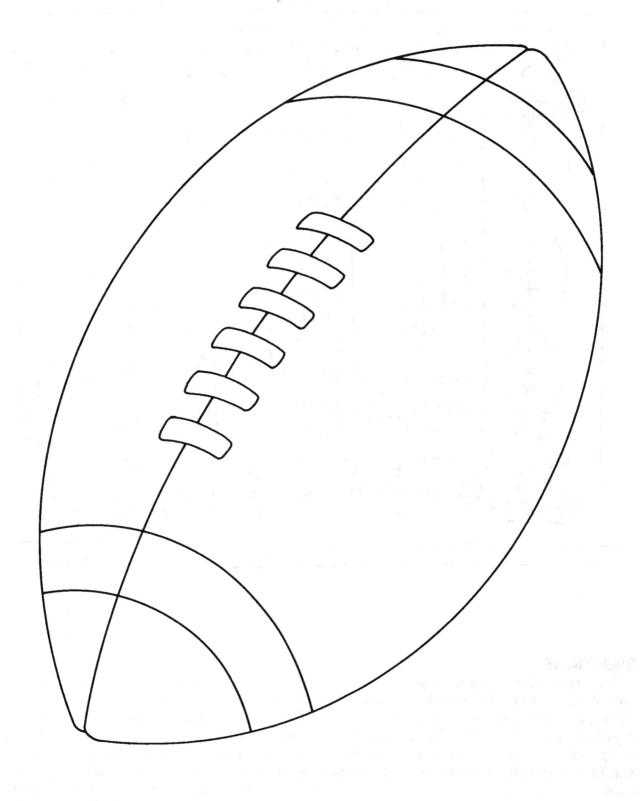

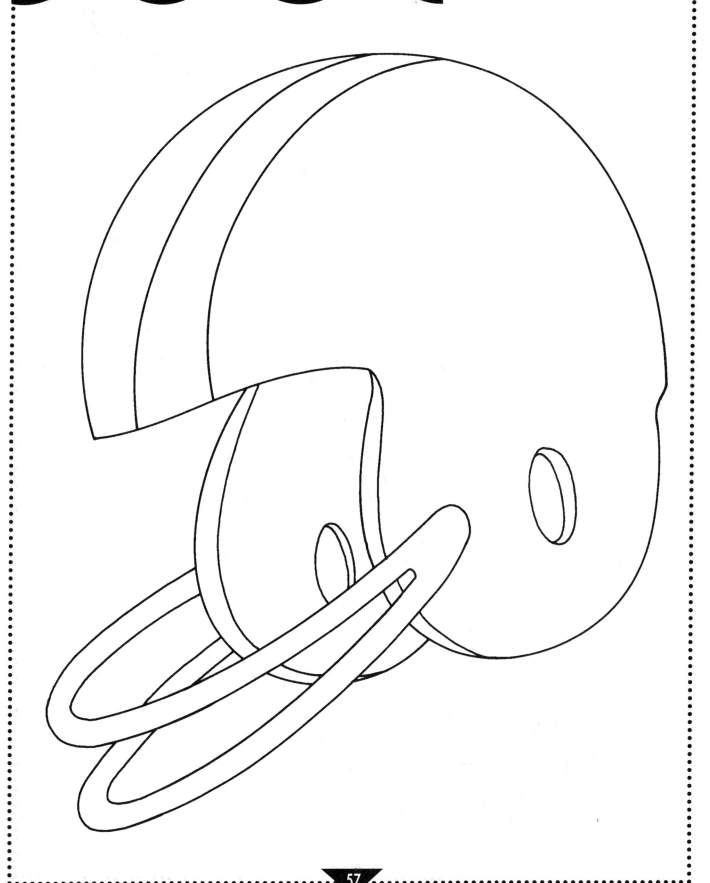

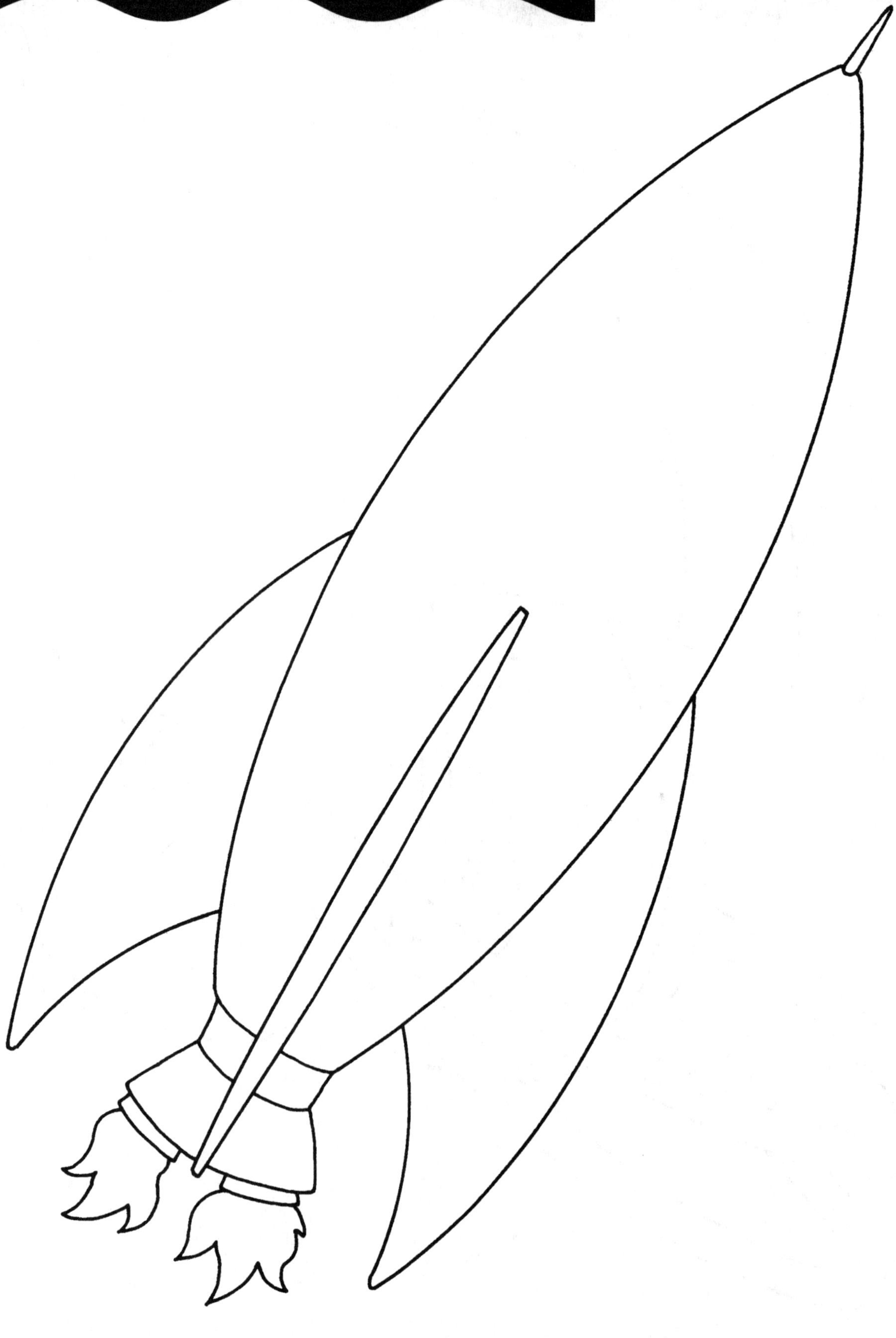

Multiplication Bulletin Board

Division Drawing

Name _____

Figure out the answer to each of the division problems below. Color the apples showing even answers red and the apples showing odd answers green.

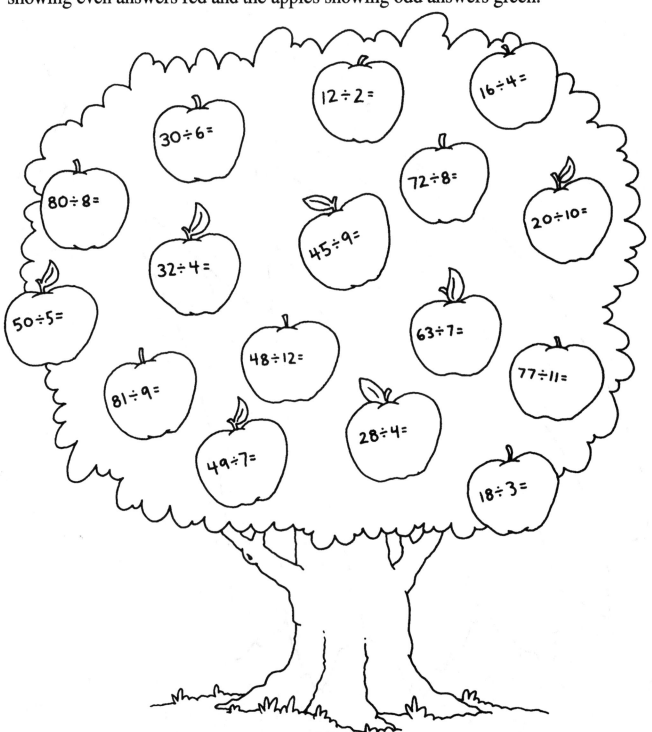

12÷2=

16÷4=

30÷6=

72÷8=

80÷8=

20÷10=

45÷9=

32÷4=

63÷7=

50÷5=

48÷12=

77÷11=

81÷9=

28÷4=

49÷7=

18÷3=

Roman Numerals

Name _____

Draw lines to match the Roman numeral on the left with its Arabic numeral on the right.

1. IV	**a.** 19
2. XVII	**b.** 33
3. XCII	**c.** 24
4. LXVI	**d.** 321
5. CCII	**e.** 64
6. VIII	**f.** 20
7. XLIX	**g.** 92
8. XXIV	**h.** 151
9. LXXXIII	**i.** 17
10. XIX	**j.** 66
11. XXXIII	**k.** 202
12. CCCXXI	**l.** 4
13. XX	**m.** 83
14. LXIV	**n.** 49
15. CLI	**o.** 8

Roman Counting

Name _____

Using Roman numerals, answer each of the questions below.

1. Anthony stopped to buy lunch at the local delicatessen. He had XIII dollars in his pocket. If milk cost II dollars, a sandwich cost IV dollars, and a piece of cake cost III dollars, how much change did Anthony receive?

_____

2. Cleo wants to take her friends to the movies. If each ticket costs VII dollars, and Cleo needs to buy four tickets, how much will it cost?

_____

3. Sarah went on a biking trip with her family. The first day, they rode XV miles. The second day, they rode XXII miles. The third day, they rode XIII miles, and the fourth day, they rode XXIV miles. How many miles did Sarah ride altogether?

_____

4. Mark worked on a farm each day one week after school. On Monday, he took care of XXXI cows. On Tuesday, he had to feed LVI chickens. On Wednesday, he cleaned the troughs for XXVII pigs. On Thursday, he put out hay for XI horses. On Friday, he herded LXXIX sheep into a pen. How many animals did Mark take care of that week?

_____

5. Beth and Ben went trick-or-treating together. On one block, they collected XX treats. On the next block, they collected XIV treats. On the third block, they received XLII treats. How many treats did they receive altogether?

_____

Roman Years

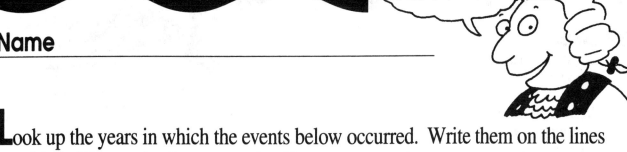

George Washington was born in MDCCXXXII.

Name _____

Look up the years in which the events below occurred. Write them on the lines provided. Then write the years using Roman numerals.

1. The Declaration of Independence is signed. _____
   _____

2. Columbus lands in the Caribbean Islands. _____
   _____

3. The San Francisco Gold Rush begins. _____
   _____

4. Napoleon comes to power, ending the French Revolution. _____
   _____

5. William Shakespeare is born. _____
   _____

6. The first man steps on the moon. _____
   _____

7. Women receive the right to vote in America. _____
   _____

8. John F. Kennedy begins his presidency. _____
   _____

9. The Civil War ends. _____
   _____

10. Magellan begins his voyage around the world. _____
    _____

Roman Races File-Folder Game

MATERIALS:

crayons or markers
scissors
glue
letter-sized file folder
modeling clay
large envelope

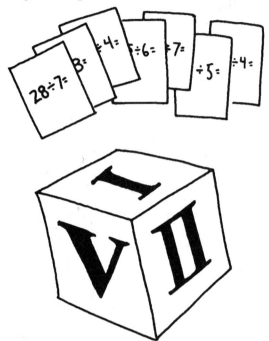

DIRECTIONS:

1. Reproduce the game board on pages 65–66 once. Color the game board, cut it out, and mount it on the inside of a letter-sized file folder.
2. Reproduce the number cube on page 67 once. Color the number cube, mount it on oaktag, and cut it out.
3. Fold the number cube along the lines. Glue the cube together as indicated.
4. Reproduce the playing cards on page 68 twice. Color the game cards, mount them on oaktag, and cut them out.
5. Reproduce the "How to Play" instructions on this page once. Glue the instructions to the front of the file folder.
6. Gather a penny, nickel, dime, and quarter to use as playing pieces.
7. Glue an envelope to the back of the file folder. Store the game board, playing cards, playing pieces, and number cube in the envelope.

HOW TO PLAY:

(for two to four players)
1. Players place their playing pieces on "Start" and place the game cards in a pile next to the game board. Players roll the number cube to see who goes first. The player with the highest number goes first.
2. The first player rolls the number cube and moves his or her playing piece the appropriate number of spaces along the game board. If a player lands on a space that has a star, he or she must draw a game card from the pile.
3. Play continues clockwise around the game board. The first player to reach "Finish" receives a bonus of X points, and the game is over. Then each player totals up the amount of points on his or her game cards. The player with the most points wins. (A player must add up his or her score correctly in order to win.)

Roman Races File-Folder Game

START

Finish

Roman Races File-Folder Game

+ V	+ X	+ XX	+ XI	+ XV
+ XIX	+ IX	+ VII	+ III	+ IV
+ XII	+ XVIII	+ II	+ XIV	+ XVI
+ I	+ XIII	+ VI	+ VIII	+ XVII
Lose V points	Lose IV points	Lose III points	Lose II points	Lose I points

Who Wants Seconds?

Name _____

Figure out the number of seconds for each of the problems below.

1. 1 minute _____

2. 1 hour _____

3. 1 day _____

4. 1 week _____

5. 1 month (30 days) _____

6. 1 year _____

7. 5 years _____

8. 1 decade _____

9. 1 century _____

NOTE: Do not include leap years in your calculations!

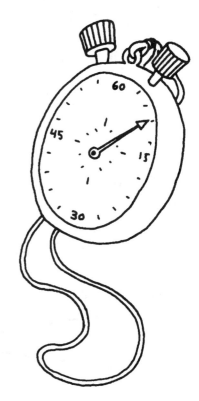

Geometry Genius

Name _____

Circle the letter in each pair that shows the correct answer.

1. parallel lines
    a.   b.

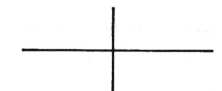

2. perpendicular lines
    a.   b.

3. intersecting lines
    a.   b.

4. right angle
    a.   b.

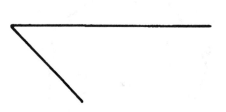

5. acute angle
    a.   b.

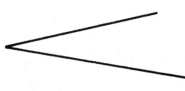

6. obtuse angle
    a.   b.

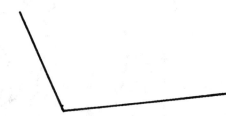

On the back of this page, write a definition for each of these terms.

Perimeter Problems

Name _____

The *perimeter* is the distance around the edge of a shape. Figure out the perimeter of each of the shapes below. Write each perimeter on the line provided.

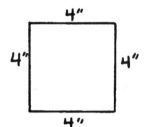

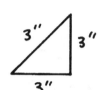

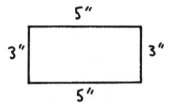

1. _____   2. _____   3. _____

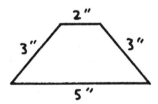

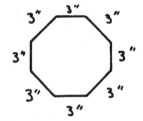

4. _____   5. _____   6. _____

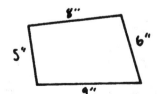

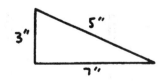

7. _____   8. _____

A Box of Chocolates

Name _____

A candy thief has been stealing chocolates from the Choco-Lot Candy Factory. Look at each of the boxes below. On the line provided, write the fraction that tells how much of each box is still filled. Then reduce each fraction to its lowest terms.

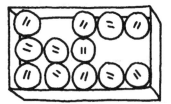

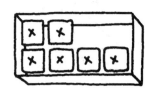

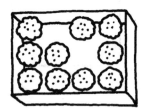

1. _____

2. _____

3. _____

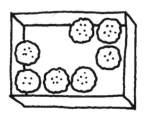

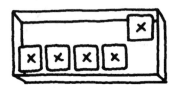

4. _____

5. _____

6. _____

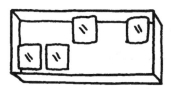

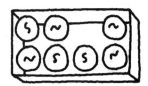

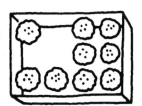

7. _____

8. _____

9. _____

Improper Fractions

Name _____

An _improper fraction_ is a fraction whose numerator is larger than its denominator.

For each improper fraction below, divide the numerator by the denominator. Write the whole number with the remainder as a fraction over the denominator. Reduce the fraction to lowest terms. The first one has been done for you.

1. 17/5 $= 3\frac{2}{5}$

$$\begin{array}{r} 3 \\ 5\overline{\smash{\big)}17} \\ 15 \\ \hline 2 \end{array}$$

2. 22/4

3. 11/2

4. 34/8

5. 16/3

6. 23/6

7. 3/2

8. 29/7

9. 8/3

Division Bingo

DIRECTIONS:

1. Reproduce each of the bingo game boards once. Cut out the boards and mount them on oaktag.

2. Reproduce the multiplication facts on page 85 once.

3. Cut out 50 small squares of construction paper to cover the spaces on the bingo boards.

4. Three students may play the game at a time. Choose one student to be the caller.

5. The caller refers to the multiplication fact sheet and calls out a random multiplication problem, such as, "Six times six equals . . ."

6. Each player scans his or her bingo board to find the equivalent division problem (such as "36 (div. by) 6").

If the player has the appropriate problem on his or her board, that player may cover the space with a piece of construction paper.

7. Remind the caller to mark off each fact after he or she has called it in order to avoid repeating any. The first player who covers a vertical, horizontal, or diagonal row on his or her game board is the winner.

8. For variations, play "Picture Frame" (players must cover the perimeters of their boards), or "Letter T" (players must cover the letter *T* on their boards), or have students cover their entire boards before ending the game.

Division Bingo

49 ÷ 7	80 ÷ 8	24 ÷ 6	66 ÷ 6	63 ÷ 9
48 ÷ 4	30 ÷ 6	54 ÷ 9	40 ÷ 5	72 ÷ 6
60 ÷ 6	48 ÷ 8	88 ÷ 8	15 ÷ 3	72 ÷ 9
45 ÷ 5	27 ÷ 9	20 ÷ 10	55 ÷ 11	21 ÷ 3
108 ÷ 9	18 ÷ 3	77 ÷ 11	6 ÷ 3	48 ÷ 12

Division Bingo

36÷6	16÷2	64÷8	72÷12	63÷9
45÷9	18÷6	35÷5	33÷3	16÷4
110÷10	40÷4	42÷7	36÷4	9÷3
81÷9	18÷9	50÷5	88÷11	100÷10
24÷2	99÷9	36÷9	32÷4	96÷8

Name _____

Fill in the shapes below to complete the long division problems.

1.
```
    △5 R4
6 ) 3□4
  -36
    3△
  -30
     △
```

2.
```
    2□△ R□
4 ) 973
   -△
    □7
   -16
    13
```

3.
```
     85 R□
△ ) 25△
  -2□
    16
   -1△
     □
```

4.
```
    3△8 R1
□ ) 1□41
  -15
    14
   -1△
    41
   -40
     1
```

5.
```
    △49 R□
8 ) 3△92
  -32
    3□
   -3□
    △2
   -7△
     □
```

6.
```
    △98 R△
7 ) 55□0
  -4△
    69
   -□3
    6△
   -△6
     4
```

Chart the Percents

Name _____

Fill in the blank spaces on the chart below.

100%

Fraction	Decimal	Percent
22/100		22%
	.54	
84/100		
		66%
	.09	
77/100		
		6%
52/100		
	.99	
1/100		
		41%
12/100		
		38%
70/100		
	.03	

8%

Sale of the Century!

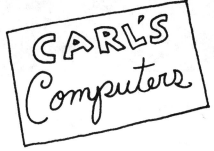

Name _____

Carl's Computers is having a going-out-of-business sale. All its computers, printers, and software have been marked down to rock-bottom prices. For the final day, Carl is slashing prices across the board.

Look at each of the items below. On the lines provided, write in the final price after the discount.

1.

$88.00
SALE 25% off

_____

2.

PRINTER $129
30% off

_____

3.

SOFTWARE $30
10% OFF

_____

4.

$650.00
40% OFF

_____

5.

$80.00
Computer Chess
60% off

_____

6.

50% off
$11.00 Discs

_____

Party Time

Name _____

Read each of the word problems below. Then use patterns to try to find out the answer to each question.

1. Randy invited two friends to his birthday party. He told each of them to invite two more people. They did, and they told their friends that they may also invite two people each. Each member of that group then invited two more friends. How many people have been invited to Randy's party?

_____

2. At the party, each person shook hands once with every other person at the party. How many handshakes were exchanged? Figure out the pattern and fill in the rest of the chart below.

Number of people at party	1	2	3	4	5	6	7	8	9	10
Number of handshakes	0	1	3	6	10					

Number of people at party	11	12	13	14
Number of handshakes				

3. Main Street Pizzeria sells a whole pizza pie for $10. A pie consists of eight slices. Buying pizza by the slice costs $1.35 per slice. If 12 kids from a baseball team want to buy pizza, and each kid can eat two slices, how much money will it cost them to buy it by the slice?

_____

How much money will it cost them to buy enough pies for everyone?

_____

How much money will they save by buying pies?

_____

Hot Potato!

Name _____

Mrs. McCracker's class is playing hot potato. To figure out who got stuck with the hot potato, read the clues below.

1. Brian passed it first.
2. Lola was the tenth person to have the potato.
3. There are 12 students in the class.
4. Robbie sat between two girls.
5. Martha touched the potato just before Eva did.
6. Each student touched the potato just once.
7. Clair sat next to Robbie.
8. Alex handed the potato to Clair.
9. Thomas sat between Jennifer and Peter.
10. Jennifer was the fifth person to touch the potato.
11. Patrick sat between two girls.
12. Greta sat next to Peter.
13. Alex touched the potato right after Brian.

Show the order in which the hot potato was passed. _____

_____

Who got stuck with the hot potato? _____

Happy Birthday to Whom?

Name _____

Read the clues below. Cross out the people who do not match the clue descriptions to help the clown figure out whose birthday it is.

1. The person has perfect vision.
2. The person is not the tallest person at the party.
3. The person is not standing next to someone wearing a hat.
4. The person is not wearing a jacket.
5. The person is not wearing a hat.

May I Take Your Order?

Name _____

The great chef Francine has forgotten to write in the names of her customers on each dinner order. Read the clues below and then fill in the appropriate name at the top of each menu.

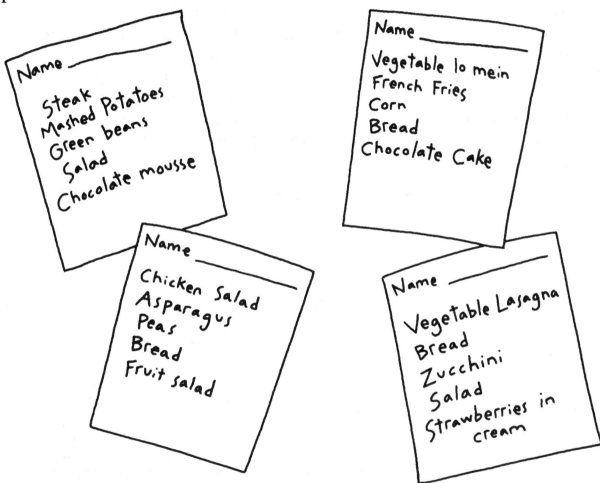

Name _____
Steak
Mashed Potatoes
Green beans
Salad
Chocolate mousse

Name _____
Vegetable lo mein
French Fries
Corn
Bread
Chocolate Cake

Name _____
Chicken Salad
Asparagus
Peas
Bread
Fruit salad

Name _____
Vegetable Lasagna
Bread
Zucchini
Salad
Strawberries in cream

1. Josh is a vegetarian.
2. Erika cannot eat dairy foods.
3. Justin does not like corn.
4. Josh does not like green vegetables.
5. Mindy does not like strawberries.
6. Mindy loves salad.
7. Erika loves desserts with fruit.
8. Mindy does not like Chinese food.
9. Justin does not eat meat.

Missing Branches

Name _____

Help the Martins fill in the missing branches of their family tree. Read the clues below. Then write each family member's name in the box in which it belongs.

1. Jill has no children.
2. Mary is Ken's sister.
3. Ken has two sisters and one brother.
4. Ethel has six grandchildren.
5. Susan is married to Ken.
6. Sam is Jill's brother.
7. Rob has two daughters.
8. Rachel is Ken's sister-in-law.
9. Susan has one child.
10. Christopher and Thomas are Tim's cousins.
11. Tim is Ken's son.
12. Becky and Megan are sisters.
13. Rob is Beth's uncle.
14. Mary is Christopher's aunt.
15. Arthur has four children.

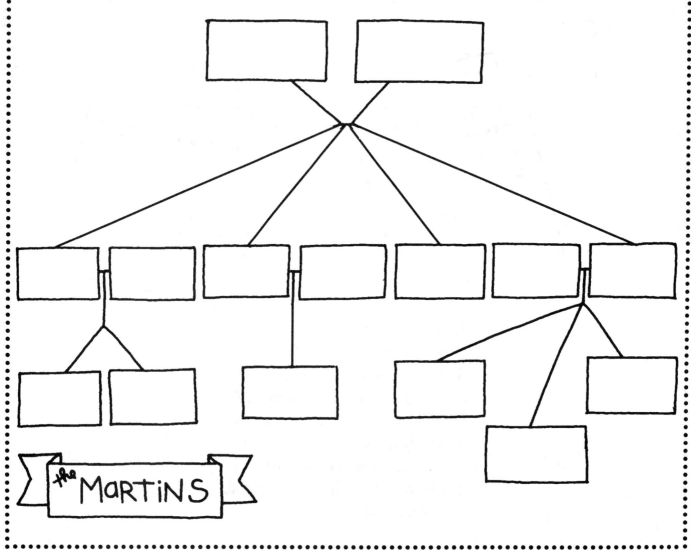

the MARTINS

1 x 0 = 0	2 x 0 = 0	3 x 0 = 0	4 x 0 = 0
1 x 1 = 1	2 x 1 = 2	3 x 1 = 3	4 x 1 = 4
1 x 2 = 2	2 x 2 = 4	3 x 2 = 6	4 x 2 = 8
1 x 3 = 3	2 x 3 = 6	3 x 3 = 9	4 x 3 = 12
1 x 4 = 4	2 x 4 = 8	3 x 4 = 12	4 x 4 = 16
1 x 5 = 5	2 x 5 = 10	3 x 5 = 15	4 x 5 = 20
1 x 6 = 6	2 x 6 = 12	3 x 6 = 18	4 x 6 = 24
1 x 7 = 7	2 x 7 = 14	3 x 7 = 21	4 x 7 = 28
1 x 8 = 8	2 x 8 = 16	3 x 8 = 24	4 x 8 = 32
1 x 9 = 9	2 x 9 = 18	3 x 9 = 27	4 x 9 = 36
1 x 10 = 10	2 x 10 = 20	3 x 10 = 30	4 x 10 = 40
1 x 11 = 11	2 x 11 = 22	3 x 11 = 33	4 x 11 = 44
1 x 12 = 12	2 x 12 = 24	3 x 12 = 36	4 x 12 = 48

5 x 0 = 0	6 x 0 = 0	7 x 0 = 0	8 x 0 = 0
5 x 1 = 5	6 x 1 = 6	7 x 1 = 7	8 x 1 = 8
5 x 2 = 10	6 x 2 = 12	7 x 2 = 14	8 x 2 = 16
5 x 3 = 15	6 x 3 = 18	7 x 3 = 21	8 x 3 = 24
5 x 4 = 20	6 x 4 = 24	7 x 4 = 28	8 x 4 = 32
5 x 5 = 25	6 x 5 = 30	7 x 5 = 35	8 x 5 = 40
5 x 6 = 30	6 x 6 = 36	7 x 6 = 42	8 x 6 = 48
5 x 7 = 35	6 x 7 = 42	7 x 7 = 49	8 x 7 = 56
5 x 8 = 40	6 x 8 = 48	7 x 8 = 56	8 x 8 = 64
5 x 9 = 45	6 x 9 = 54	7 x 9 = 63	8 x 9 = 72
5 x 10 = 50	6 x 10 = 60	7 x 10 = 70	8 x 10 = 80
5 x 11 = 55	6 x 11 = 66	7 x 11 = 77	8 x 11 = 88
5 x 12 = 60	6 x 12 = 72	7 x 12 = 84	8 x 12 = 96

9 x 0 = 0	10 x 0 = 0	11 x 0 = 0	12 x 0 = 0
9 x 1 = 9	10 x 1 = 10	11 x 1 = 11	12 x 1 = 12
9 x 2 = 18	10 x 2 = 20	11 x 2 = 22	12 x 2 = 24
9 x 3 = 27	10 x 3 = 30	11 x 3 = 33	12 x 3 = 36
9 x 4 = 36	10 x 4 = 40	11 x 4 = 44	12 x 4 = 48
9 x 5 = 45	10 x 5 = 50	11 x 5 = 55	12 x 5 = 60
9 x 6 = 54	10 x 6 = 60	11 x 6 = 66	12 x 6 = 72
9 x 7 = 63	10 x 7 = 70	11 x 7 = 77	12 x 7 = 84
9 x 8 = 72	10 x 8 = 80	11 x 8 = 88	12 x 8 = 96
9 x 9 = 81	10 x 9 = 90	11 x 9 = 99	12 x 9 = 108
9 x 10 = 90	10 x 10 = 100	11 x 10 = 110	12 x 10 = 120
9 x 11 = 99	10 x 11 = 110	11 x 11 = 121	12 x 11 = 132
9 x 12 = 108	10 x 12 = 120	11 x 12 = 132	12 x 12 = 144

Weights and Measurements

STANDARD	METRIC

Measurements of Length

STANDARD	METRIC
12 inches = 1 foot	10 millimeters = 1 centimeter
3 feet = 1 yard	100 centimeters = 1 meter
5, 280 feet = 1 mile	1,000 meters = 1 kilometer

Liquid Measurements

STANDARD	METRIC
16 fluid ounces = 1 pint	10 milliliters = 1 centiliter
2 pints = 1 quart	100 centiliters = 1 liter
4 quarts = 1 gallon	

Measurements of Weight

STANDARD	METRIC
16 ounces = 1 pound	10 milligrams = 1 centigram
2,000 pounds = 1 ton	100 centigrams = 1 gram
	1,000 grams = 1 kilogram
	1,000 kilograms = 1 metric ton

Standard/Metric Conversions

1 inch = 2.54 centimeters	1 centimeter = .039 inches
1 yard = .91 meters	1 meter = 1.09 yards
1 mile = 1.61 kilometers	1 kilometer = .62 miles

Roman Numerals

one	I	eleven	XI	thirty	XXX
two	II	twelve	XII	forty	XL
three	III	thirteen	XIII	fifty	L
four	IV	fourteen	XIV	sixty	LX
five	V	fifteen	XV	seventy	LXX
six	VI	sixteen	XVI	eighty	LXXX
seven	VII	seventeen	XVII	ninety	XC
eight	VIII	eighteen	XVIII	one hundred	C
nine	IX	nineteen	XIX	five hundred	D
ten	X	twenty	XX	one thousand	M

1st
Place
Timed Tests

Presented
to
For magical math skills

PRESENTED
to

outstanding
student

MATHLETE

Teacher

Date

Presented to

_____

for improving by

_____   _____
Teacher   **Date**

Answers

page 6
1. 34 feet
2. 2,080 cubic feet
3. 43 pounds; 20 kilograms
4. 1,200 square feet; 320 square feet; 2,250 square feet; 100 square feet
5. 13.4, 16, 19; 48.4

page 8
Jessica—90
Sam—88.8
Alex—91.6
Denise—90.2
Kate—98.2
Ray—87.6
Jamie—93.6
Chris—83.6

class average—90.45

page 9
1. 1/4 foot
2. 12 inches; 1/3 yard
3. 60 inches; 152.4 centimeters
4. 72 inches; 6 feet; 2 yards
5. 2,000 yards
6. 3,622.5 meters
7. 5 1/4 miles
8. 45,000 meters; 15,000 meters

page 10
1. $18
2. $18
3. $216
4. $6, $12, $18, $24, $30
5. $24, $60, $72, $84; n + 12
6. n + 3

page 11
1. each number is multiplied by itself to get the next answer in the series
2. (n x 3) + 1
3. 81, 243, 729, 2,187
4. 48 feet high
5. 4,224

page 12
1. 23,725
2. 79.5%
3. 1/16
4. vegetable salad
5. 205
6. Ted 11:1, Ned 12:1
7. 38; 19; 76

page 13
1. 30
2. 60
3. 15
4. 10
5. 10; 30; 0
6. 9

page 14
answers will vary

page 16
1. 4
2. 8; 12; 16
3. 1 1/2
4. 20
5. 128
6. 48

page 19
1. 4 1/2 yards
2. 4 5/8 yards
3. 2 buttons
4. yes
5. 1 yard; 1 yard
6. answers will vary; possible answer: 4 shirts; sizes 1, 2, 3, 5
7. 120
8. 4 1/4 yards

page 20
1. 2 pieces 21" x 17" or 1 piece 42" x 34"
2. 2 boards at 3' long x 12" deep
3. 48; 4
4. 10 yards for both windows
5. 2 quarts
6. 20'

page 21
1. 72 6' boards; 72 9' boards
2. one 6', 1" x 6" board and one 10', 1" x 6" board; $4.50
3. 3; yes; 1/2 board
4. $49.35 (round off to $50.00); $52.50
5. no; buy a 1" x 3" board at 10' long and saw off 1'

page 22
1. answers will vary
2. yes; yes
3. buy a 5' x 7' rug and cut out areas for the toilet and sink
4. answers will vary
5. 432
6. answers will vary

Answers

page 23

1. 100-ounce size
2. 201 sinkfuls
3. .06 cents for 46 sinkfuls; .04 cents for 201 sinkfuls
4. 1/2 ounce
5. $7.80; $5.46
6. 5

page 24

1. car 1—$892.50; car 2—$535.50; the first car
2. no; car 1—4,785; car 2—$4,471
3. $15,540; $17,760
4. 8
5. $14,520; $403
6. $1,920

page 25

1. 56
2. 6.6; 7
3. 32; 16
4. 25; 75
5. 43 : 1
6. 111

page 26

1. yes; $234.33
2. $1.25; $19.52
3.

4. 16 7/8 miles
5. yes
6. 25%, 20%, 10%, 30%, 15%; orange

page 27–28

Check #	Date	Transaction	Debit	Credit	Balance
					1,000.00
	5/1	Withdrawal ATM	20.00		980.00
120	5/10	to Dr. Bean	60.00		920.00
	5/16	Deposit		200.00	1120.00
	5/20	Withdrawal	20.00		1100.00
121	5/24	to Electric Company	21.45		1078.55
122	5/25	to Telephone Company	63.95		1014.60
123	6/1	?	650.00		364.60
	6/1	Withdrawal ATM	60.00		304.60
124	6/10	to Mary Lane	45.23		259.37
	6/16	Deposit		92.37	351.74
	6/20	Withdrawal	100.00		251.74
125	6/29	to Electric Company	23.72		228.02
126	6/30	to Telephone Company	54.63		173.39
	7/1	Withdrawal	20.00		153.39
	7/2	Deposit		80.00	233.39
	7/6	Withdrawal	60.00		173.39

page 29

1. 80%
2. pop
3.

UP
Put Your Hand in Mine
Love Is Grand
Time to Cry
Hairy Days and Nights

STAYED THE SAME
Ray of Sunshine

DOWN
Oh, Baby!
Shades
Heartbreak
Time Outdoors
Riding in My Car

Answers

4.

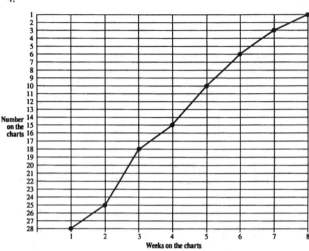

Number on the charts / Weeks on the charts

5. 4
6. 10%; 40%; 50%

page 30
1. 20
2. no
3. 72
4. 60-minute
5. 50%; 20%; 15%; 15%
6. Sam has 34, Bill has 17, Kathy has 2, Hal has 16

page 31

1.
2. 17 19 28 37 39
3. 77 78 87 88 98

4.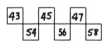
5. 72 74 82 83 84 92 94
6. 78 79 89 90 97 98

7. 43 45 47 54 56 58
8.   14 23 32 41

9.   60 69 70 79 89 90 100
10. 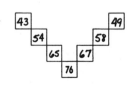 43 49 54 58 65 67 76

page 34
1–4. Answers will vary
5. $14.32
6–10. Answers will vary
11. 1,235
12. 135

page 44

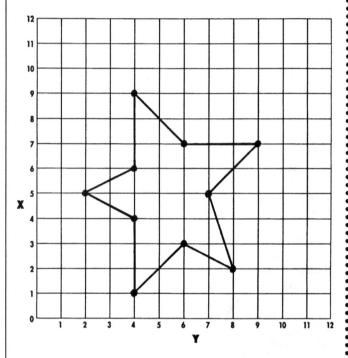

page 45

Number	Place Value					Word Version
	Ten thousands	Thousands	Hundreds	Tens	Ones	
1. 4,809		4	8	0	9	four thousand eight hundred nine
2. 403			4	0	3	four hundred three
3. 34,965	3	4	9	6	5	thirty-four thousand nine hundred sixty-five
4. 35,806	3	5	8	0	6	thirty-five thousand eight hundred six
5. 3,001		3	0	0	1	three thousand one
6. 7,906		7	9	0	6	seven thousand nine hundred six
7. 6,022		6	0	2	2	six thousand twenty-two
8. 63,840	6	3	8	4	0	sixty-three thousand eight hundred forty
9. 298			2	9	8	two hundred ninety-eight
10. 59				5	9	fifty-nine

page 46

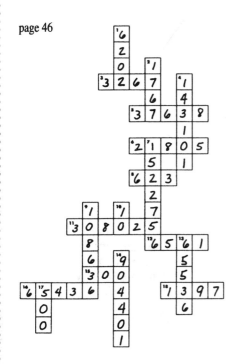

page 47

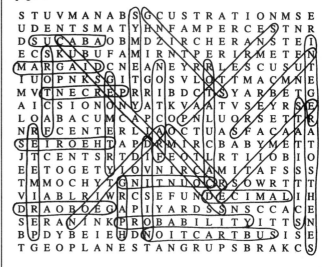

page 48

The correct row has the following answers: $1748 \div 46 = 38$; $6 \times 2 \times 3 \times 1 = 36$; $6\ 1/2 \times 4\ 3/4 = 30.9$; $192 \div 6 = 32$; $3{,}687 - 3{,}652 = 35$; square root of $1{,}089 = 33$

page 50

1. 75%
2. 41 minutes, 45 seconds
3. 2,006; 87,600
4. n + 1, n + 2, n + 3, etc.; 66 years old
5. 103 years, 10 months, 6 days
6. 4 : 3

page 51

Answers

page 52

1. 230 : 460, or 1 : 2
2. 39 : 78, or 1 : 2
3. 117 : 120
4. 98 : 66, or 49 : 33
5. 3 : 5
6. 30 : 60, or 1 : 2

page 53

1. 6	51. 27
2. 36	52. 132
3. 32	53. 36
4. 9	54. 21
5. 0	55. 70
6. 45	56. 0
7. 49	57. 48
8. 12	58. 99
9. 100	59. 63
10. 24	60. 60
11. 27	61. 0
12. 42	62. 88
13. 45	63. 12
14. 11	64. 40
15. 21	65. 80
16. 72	66. 24
17. 72	67. 63
18. 22	68. 70
19. 20	69. 60
20. 99	70. 18
21. 24	71. 108
22. 84	72. 88
23. 8	73. 15
24. 18	74. 24
25. 0	75. 10
26. 16	76. 0
27. 66	77. 8
28. 35	78. 33
29. 2	79. 18
30. 12	80. 90
31. 77	81. 144
32. 50	82. 40
33. 56	83. 8
34. 120	84. 40
35. 81	85. 108
36. 0	86. 42
37. 54	87. 77
38. 48	88. 16
39. 44	89. 4
40. 12	90. 20
41. 7	91. 66
42. 96	92. 9
43. 110	93. 56
44. 30	94. 40
45. 14	95. 28
46. 28	96. 10
47. 30	97. 14
48. 5	98. 110
49. 24	99. 48
50. 55	100. 36

page 60

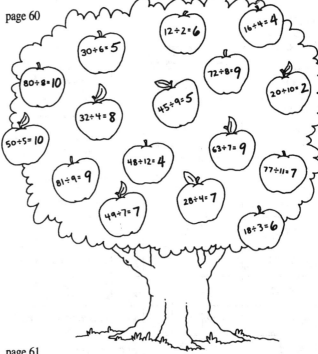

page 61

1. l	9. m
2. i	10. a
3. g	11. b
4. j	12. d
5. k	13. f
6. o	14. e
7. n	15. h
8. c	

page 62

1. IV dollars
2. XXVIII dollars
3. LXXIV
4. CCIV
5. LXXVI

page 63

1. 1776; MDCCLXXVI	6. 1969; MCMLXIX
2. 1492; MCDXCII	7. 1920; MCMXX
3. 1849; MDCCCXLIX	8. 1961; MCMLXI
4. 1799; MDCCXCIX	9. 1865; MDCCCLXV
5. 1564; MDLXIV	10. 1519; MDXIX

page 69

1. 60
2. 3,600
3. 86,400
4. 604,800
5. 2,592,000
6. 31,536,000
7. 157,680,000
8. 315,360,000
9. 3,153,600,000

page 70

1. a
2. b
3. a
4. a
5. b
6. b

1. parallel lines—two or more lines that do not intersect
2. perpendicular lines—lines that intersect and form right angles
3. intersecting lines—two or more lines that cross over one another
4. right angle—a 90° angle formed by two perpendicular lines
5. acute angle—an angle that measures less than 90°
6. obtuse angle—an angle that measures more than 90° but less than 180°

page 71

1. 16"
2. 9"
3. 16"
4. 13"
5. 24"
6. 30"
7. 28"
8. 15"

page 72

1. 4/5
2. 3/4
3. 5/6
4. 7/12
5. 2/3
6. 1/2
7. 2/5
8. 7/8
9. 3/4

page 73

1. 3 2/5
2. 5 1/2
3. 5 1/2
4. 4 1/4
5. 5 1/3
6. 3 5/6
7. 1 1/2
8. 4 1/7
9. 2 2/3

page 77

1. 65 R4
   6)394
   -36
    34
   -30
     4

2. 243 R1
   4)973
   -8
    17
   -16
    13

3. 85 R1
   3)256
   -24
    16
   -15
     1

4. 328 R1
   5)1641
   -15
    14
   -10
    41
   -40
     1

5. 449 R0
   8)3592
   -32
    39
   -32
    72
   -72
     0

6. 798 R4
   7)5590
   -49
    69
   -63
    60
   -56
     4

page 78

Fraction	Decimal	Percent
22/100	.22	22%
54/100	.54	54%
84/100	.84	84%
66/100	.66	66%
9/100	.09	9%
77/100	.77	77%
6/100	.06	6%
52/100	.52	52%
99/100	.99	99%
1/100	.01	1%
41/100	.41	41%
12/100	.12	12%
38/100	.38	38%
70/100	.70	70%
3/100	.03	3%

Answers

page 79
1. $66
2. $90.30
3. $27
4. $390
5. $32
6. $5.50

page 80
1. 14
2.

Number of people at party	1	2	3	4	5	6	7	8	9	10
Number of handshakes	0	1	3	6	10	15	21	28	36	45

Number of people at party	11	12	13	14
Number of handshakes	55	66	78	91

3. $32.40; $30.00; $2.40

page 81
Brian, Alex, Clair, Robbie, Jennifer, Thomas, Peter, Greta, Patrick, Lola, Martha, Eva; Eva

page 82
The man wearing shorts

page 83
Mindy, Josh, Erika, Justin

page 84

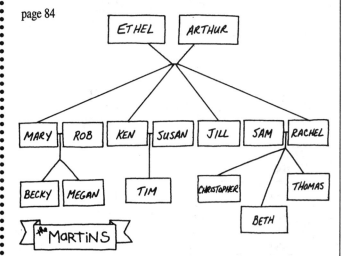